The Forgotten Irish

Seán Carney

Connaught Man

The history of a South Yorkshire Irish mining community

Black Tree Publishing

Cover photograph 'Pit Brow Girls at Work', circa 19th century; photographer unknown. From Mick Bowyer's 'The Coal Shop Collection Volume 2'.

Illustration 'The Connaught Man', by Steven Taylor, Illustrated London News (www.illustratedlondonnews.co.uk)

Cover Design: Charlotte Klingholz, London
Printed and published by Black Tree Publishing, Kingston upon Hull

ISBN: 978-0-9572954-1-4

This book is dedicated to my father and mother Hugh Fergus and Doris Eliza Carney, Stalwarts of Maltby's Irish mining community.

May they rest in peace.

ACKNOWLEDGEMENTS

I wish to acknowledge and thank the following for their kind support and encouragement shown to me over the past four years since I first embarked on the road to writing the history of Maltby's Irish mining community, without whom this humble story would not have been told.

The late Maggie Quinn, nee Carney, my aunt: Mounttcharles County Donegal, who unwittingly sowed the seeds of this book.

My wife, Maire, for her constant advice, for listening to endless stories of Maltby's characters and for putting up with my unsociable hours sat in front of a computer.

My children Mary Bridget, Sarah Ethna, Deirdre and Padraig, and sons-in Law Craig Anderson Chris Johnston. Thanks to Dave Stanford.

To my old pal Jim Regan for his advice and help, for his invaluable organization, his contacts, and putting up with my constant questions and queries.

John Davies, grandson of County Galway miner Paddy Gibney, for sharing his unique collection of old photographs of Maltby's Irish community and also for his knack of finding people, phone numbers and responding selflessly to my emails and queries.

Thanks also Julia Stuart: to Mick McCann: Paddy Connolly: Mick Connole: Geoff Wallis: Liam Hyland, editor of The Donegal Times: Lee Whitney and Ellen Crain at Butte Silverbow Archives in Montana, USA: Father O'Neill at Saint Patrick's Church in Butte: Bridie Durkan (nee Carroll): Tim Miskell: the late Frank Keetley RIP: Pete Clements and his Yorkshire Main website: Noel Gallagher, of Mountcharles, County Donegal: Pat Conaghan and his book, The Great Famine In South West Donegal: the North Western Region Register Office in Letterkenny, County Donegal: David Sutton: The Tickhill and District Local History: Maltby Library: Rotherham Library: Astley Green Colliery Museum: Jennifer Kelly at the North of England Institute of Mining and Mechanical Engineers: English Heritage and Conisbrough Castle: Robert Finnigan at the Leeds Diocese Catholic Archives: Maltby Historical Society: the late Rene Mulhearn publican Mountcharles: Mary Hughes: Nellie Gallagher: Martin Gildea Jr: Joe McNicholas: and Rotherweb Local History: Dr Charles Kelham principle archivist Doncaster Archives for eviction image at Denaby Main. Peter Smith at Skanska Cementation Ltd Doncaster. Thyssen Shaft Sinking & Drilling, Germany.

INTRODUCTION

The coal mining industry in the 19th century was a model of British entrepreneurial skill, which coincided with the industrial revolution. Vast Fortunes were accumulated by often despotic intransigent mine owners. Landowners also shared in immense fortunes in the form of royalties from the coal seams which lay beneath their vast swaths of land. One wealthy titled landowner, admitted that he had performed no services to mankind whatsoever in exchange for royalties from the land his estate was sat on.

Society in the nineteenth and early twentieth century was inextricably dependent on coal. Coal was the stuff of steelmaking, heavy industry, ship and bridge building, railways, power stations, domestic and street lighting and lucrative exports to foreign parts.

In the early days this ignoble industry and so called Christian nation, required that girls, boys and women, should work in slave-like conditions in a pitch black underworld tethered like beasts to coal tubs by chains which they pulled along on all fours in order to create wealth for their masters and the nation.

Men fared little better working day after day, year in year out, crawling their back and sides stripped to the waist in coal seams no more than two feet high. Gruesome deadly accidents and death by gassing and explosion were regularly accepted hazards of the industry.

Although made illegal in the mid nineteenth century, tyrannical Gang masters still lingered on into the twentieth century to add to their misery.

Shamefully coal was still being won by pick and shovel in the many pits throughout the land, and not until 1947 with the advent of nationalization, mechanization, and a strong union did conditions in the majority of the U.K. mines begin to improve.

Contents

CHAPTER ONE
WHAT LIES BENEATH

MY father, a bold, dark wavy-haired handsome native of Donegal, was never one for great demonstrations of affection.

But every day of his working life, as he readied himself for another shift at the coalface, he would pull on his coat in the hallway of our terraced house in the heart of Yorkshire, some 400 miles from his homeland.

Without exception, whether it was a day, afternoon or night shift my father was preparing for, my mother would always be by his side, anxiously waiting to say her goodbyes.

He would gently kiss her, bless himself and, without daring to look back, walk out the door to start his shift.

They were the only times I ever saw mam and dad kiss in their 55-plus years of marriage.

But it was no doubt a scene repeated in scores of terraced homes across Maltby and beyond.

Few words, if any, were said or needed, but in such a fleeting, tender moment the very essence of life – hope, fear, love and death – was played out behind every door of every miner's home the length and breadth of Britain, if not the world.

Because no matter where they called home, as every miner left behind their loved ones in readiness to plunge into the darkness and far, far into the bowels of the earth, the only certainty was that not one of those brave souls could be certain they would ever see daylight or their families again.

Writing in 1937, George Orwell provided a brilliant description of the "savage work" of coal mining[1].

He wrote: "The place is like Hell, or at least my mental picture of Hell. Most things one imagines in Hell are there – heat, noise, confusion, darkness, foul air and, above all, unbearable cramped spaces. Everything except fire, for there is no fire down there except the feeble beams of Davy Lamps and electric torches which scarcely penetrate the clouds of coal dust...

"It is impossible to watch the 'fillers' at work without feeling a pang of envy for their toughness. It is a dreadful job that they do, an almost superhuman job by the standard of an ordinary person.

"The fillers look and work as though they were made of iron. They really do look like hammered iron statues, under the smooth coat of coal dust which clings to them from head to foot."

I often think about these "superhumans" like my father, these iron men coated in coal dust, for, in my opinion, the achievements of the Irish mineworkers in Britain were nothing short of remarkable.

Many, like my dad, had been forced to emigrate from Ireland, a country that was unable to provide for its young in the early 20th century (author James Joyce perhaps described it best when he likened Ireland at that time to "the old sow that eats her farrow"; a country that was its own unwitting oppressor).

Arriving in a religious and racially intolerant Britain with just the clothes they stood up in, these Irish immigrants were penniless and without skills.

Many seized the opportunity which mining, for all its inherent dangers, offered them.

Pitting their lives and wits against nature 3,000ft below ground for hours on end, day after day, month after month, year after year, required great courage, integrity and resolve – characteristics they possessed in abundance.

They forged their own communities among the million-plus miners in more than 3,000 coalmines scattered throughout the UK, from Scotland down to Kent, from the mid-19th century to the early 1960s. They toiled for most of their often relatively short lives alongside their British workmates in some of the most appalling, dehumanising conditions imaginable. Gassing, explosions, lung disease and gruesome accidents were no exaggerated hazard in the life of a miner, coupled with the fact their work was overseen and controlled more often than not by despotic, greedy mine and landowners.

As Michael Pollard wrote in his book, The Hardest Work Under Heaven, coal mining was simply "an affront to human nature, comparable perhaps to the Inquisition".[2]

The history of Irish immigrants who built Britain's canals, roads and rail network, who toiled on the construction sites in our cities, especially from the 1950s onwards, has been well documented. They are often referred to as "the men who built Britain".

Their struggles and hardships are poignant and worthy of gratitude, for their contribution to the building of a nation was invaluable.

But, in my mind, the real men who built Britain have been largely ignored. They were the thousands of forgotten Irish, the immigrants like my father who on arrival in England picked up their shovels, plunged the depths and mined for coal.

Through their efforts, grit and determination, they not only raised families and built communities, but shaped a country and ultimately an empire that stretched to all four corners of the globe.

As we were taught in school, the empire was built on coal. Without it and the miners to get it, Britain as we know it, for better or for worse, could not have existed.

Orwell again perhaps summed it up best when he wrote: "Practically everything we do, from eating an ice to crossing the Atlantic, and from baking a loaf to writing a novel, involves the use of coal, directly or indirectly. Whatever may be happening on the surface, the hacking and shoveling have got to continue without a pause, or at any rate without pausing for more than a few weeks at the most. But on the whole we are not aware of it; we all know that we 'must have coal', but we seldom or never remember what coal-getting involves. You could quite easily drive a car right across the north of England and never once remember that hundreds of feet below the road you are on, the miners are hacking at the coal. Yet in a sense it is the miners who are driving your car forward. Their lamp-lit world down there is as necessary to the daylight world above as the root is to the flower."[3]

Most industrial workers left no memorial, save for the products of their labour, which for pitmen were hidden deep below ground.

Hopefully, this humble chronicle will in some small way help shine a light on the darkness that has continued to cast its shadow over these subterranean heroes long after their own working lives at the coalface have come to an end.

---

1 George Orwell, The Road To Wigan Pier, Penguin Modern Classics (2001), p18-31

2 Michael Pollard, The Hardest Work Under Heaven: The Life And Death Of The British Coal Miner, Hutchinson (1986), p21

3 Orwell, loc. Cit.

CHAPTER TWO
A SHORT HISTORY LESSON

THE STORY of the "forgotten Irish" is inextricably linked to the history of Ireland and England, and in particular the great social and political changes that took place in the latter half of the 19th century and the early part of the 20th century.

For their story to be truly understood and appreciated it is perhaps necessary to provide some context with a brief account of Ireland's much troubled past and its often fraught relationship with England.

At the start of Queen Victoria's reign in 1837, England was mainly an agricultural nation, but by the time of her death in 1901 more than three-quarters of the population lived in towns or cities.

New inventions and faster machines developed as a result of the Industrial Revolution, which fuelled the growth of industrial cities.

New factories were built and trade flourished as Great Britain controlled vast swathes of the globe and became the most powerful nation on earth.

The standard of living of some members of the working population began to increase relatively fast as a result. Between 1860 and 1914, real wages doubled[1] and for the first time a significant number began to enjoy leisure time. Some money, although not much, was available for more than the essentials of food, housing and clothing. While it was only a minority who became obscenely rich on the back of Britain's progress and the working man's toil, it was perhaps little wonder so many Irish eyes cast envious glances eastwards to a 'golden age' taking root across the Irish Sea.

For the men and women of the Emerald Isle had endured little else but pain and hardship, oppression and exploitation ever since Henry II crossed the Irish Sea from England with his armies in 1171.

Nearly 400 years later, in 1541, Henry VIII became the first King of England also to pronounce himself King of Ireland and at the beginning of the 17th century, a sizeable group of immigrant Protestant landowners developed and took ownership of Irish land while a system of laws gradually established Protestant supremacy over native Catholics.

There followed centuries of what even the most committed Anglophile would accept was often merciless exploitation and cruelty, some deliberate, much through sheer negligence.

A Royal Commission, set up by the British Government in 1843 to look at the land question in Ireland, was chaired by the Earl of Devon.

He reported that for the Irish labourer and his family "their pig and a manure heap constitute their only property"[2].

The historian Cecil Woodham-Smith said the landlords' abuse of their powers created an Irish peasantry that was "one of the most destitute in Europe"[3], with millions either driven from their lands or driven to their deaths.

It was during the reign of Queen Victoria that Ireland suffered the terrible famines of the mid-19th century when the potato crops failed and an estimated one million people starved to death.

As many as two million Irish chose to emigrate to flee starvation and in search of a better life, to America or to Britain which, in sharp contrast to Ireland, was undergoing such a period of rapid change, growth and, for some at least, prosperity.

The sheer scale of the Irish diaspora is emphasised by the fact while Ireland's population almost doubled between 1780 and 1851 to about seven million[4], it subsequently, thanks largely to mortality and emigration, spiralled steeply and spectacularly downwards, so much so that by the 1930s, just a few years after my father and scores of other Irish immigrants had first arrived in Maltby in Yorkshire with the promise of a lifetime's work and decent pay, the population in his homeland was little more than four million.

In industrial England, the poor Irish immigrant had been all but welcomed with open arms, for he was prepared to work for wages far below the English norm.

The vast majority of migrants being skilled with only the shovel, drifted into the most menial and yet most arduous forms of employment; canal and railway building, dock work, harvesting, in the mills, on construction sites and, perhaps the toughest of them all, the coalmines.

But it was not that the Irish were stupid or barbarians. The

pioneering social researcher Henry Mayhew, in his groundbreakii.
survey of the poor of London conducted in the middle of the 19ᵗ
century, remarked upon "their generosity, their powers of speech
and quickness of apprehension"⁵.

Nor was it the fact they were cheap and unfussy when it came to
their chosen line of work that made them so important to Britain's
burgeoning prosperity. Quite simply, the English could not keep up
the pace. Of the Irish, the Marxist historian EP Thompson said: "The
heavy manual occupations at the base of English society required
a spendthrift expense of sheer physical energy - an alternation of
incisive labour and boisterous relaxation which belongs to the
pre-industrial labour rhythms, and for which the English artisan
or weaver was unsuited both by reason of his weakened physique
and Puritan temperament. This Irish labour was essential for the
industrial revolution, not only because it was 'cheap' but because
the Irish peasantry had escaped the imprint of Baxter and Wesley.
"Demoralised in Ireland by a subsistence economy (by which they
were reduced to semi slavery to the farmers in return for the use
of a potato patch) they had acquired a reputation for lethargy and
fecklessness. Energy was no asset in a land where the good tenant
was penalised by doubling his rent. In England they were capable
of astonishing feats, showing willingness alacrity and perseverance
in the severest and irksome and most disagreeable kinds of coarse
labour."⁶

Similarly, in 1836 at a Birmingham tribunal, an employer gave
evidence. He said: 'The Irish labourer will work any time. I consider
them very valuable and we could not do without them; by treating
them kindly they will do anything for you. An Englishman could not
do the work they do. When you push them they have a willingness to
oblige, which the English have not. They would die under anything
before they would be beat; they would go at hard work till they drop.
Before a man should excel them, it is literally true that they would
die before they would be beat.

"They require more looking after. They talk more at work, they
are good humored themselves and work best for good humored
employers who encourage them to mutual emulation. At times they
are more violent and irritable but they are less stubborn, sullen,
self-willed, than the English. Their generosity and impulsiveness

was easily put on. In his own country he is notoriously lazy in the extreme. After crossing the channel he becomes a model of laboriousness and enterprise. Paid at piece-work or the going rate, on the docks or navvying, they are tempted to over-work themselves and to ruin their health and constitution in a few years."[7]

For those Irish who remained behind in their homeland, the Great Famine was to prove a watershed, not only in the social and economic history of their country but also in its political landscape.

Perhaps not surprisingly, it was during Victoria's reign that the first real stirrings of Irish nationalism were felt.

Hunger and poverty have always been powerful agents when it comes to revolutions and the Great Famine proved no exception.

Both for native Irishmen and those joining the mass exodus, it became a rallying point for the nationalist movement.

John Mitchel, one of the leading political writers in Ireland at the time, wrote: "The Almighty, indeed, sent the potato blight, but the English created the Famine".

Resentment towards the English was so inflamed that by the start of the 20th century the movement for Irish independence was a growing force and could no longer be ignored.

However, the outbreak of the First World War in 1914 delayed the implementation of legislation that would have restored the Dublin parliament.

In 1916, nationalists staged the Easter Rising, proclaiming an independent Irish Republic, but the rising was crushed and the British executed the leaders, sparking outrage among the Irish people.

Led by Eamonn De Valera, in 1919 the nationalist movement Sinn Fein set up a Dublin assembly and again proclaimed Irish independence. A guerilla campaign by the Irish Republican Army against British forces began with heavy casualties on both sides.

The Irish Free State came into being at the end of 1922, following the signing of a treaty with England. Under the treaty, the Free State became an independent dominion of the British crown, partitioned from Northern Ireland, which remained part of the UK.

What followed was a bitter and traumatic civil war which lasted until 1923, with nationalists, such as de Valera, opposing the treaty because it did not grant full Irish independence.

Over the next nine years, under the conservative rule of William Cosgrave, the Irish Free State set about consolidating the country's economy and institutions.

In 1932, de Valera and his new party, Fianna Fail, led a government and introduced various measures to eliminate lingering British influence, adopting a constitution that jettisoned any reference to the British crown and containing a territorial claim over Northern Ireland.

Five years later and Ireland abolished the Irish Free State and proclaimed Eire, Gaelic for Ireland, as a sovereign, independent, democratic state.

My father's arrival in Britain in the 1920s coincided then with tumultuous events in Irish – and British - history as years of resentment and rebellion came to a head and the political situation in Ireland was transformed.

However, with or without the Brits, Ireland even in the 1930s and 1940s remained a very poor country.

The great majority of the people were living in the countryside. Dublin, the capital, had a maximum population of about half a million people and contained some of the worst slums in Europe, with many people living in squalid tenements without even the most basic of facilities.

Rural folk fared little better. In the 1930s, the majority of Ireland's population occupied small agricultural holdings, but wages were low for a farm labourer, amounting to less than 15 shillings a week. Most family farms were without running water or electricity, sanitation was poor and there were few modern conveniences.

In such circumstances, is it any wonder thousands of Irish continued to look to England for a better life?

There is no shortage of irony in that; the country that had infected their homeland through generations of neglect, misrule and repression was to thousands upon thousands of Irishmen still the Promised Land.

---

1 Kenneth O' Morgan, The Oxford History Of Britain, Oxford University Press (1993), p536

2 Cecil Woodham-Smith, The Great Hunger: Ireland 1845-49, Signet (1991), p24

3 ibid

4 O' Morgan, op cit, p477

5 Henry Mayhew, London Labour And The London Poor (1851) Digital edition, created from the 1861 edition. Permanent URL: *http://hdl.Handle. Net/10427/53837*. From the Edwin C. Bolles papers (MS004), Digital Collections and Archives, Tufts University, Medford, MA.

6 EP Thompson, The Making Of The English Working Class, Victor Gollancz Ltd, (1963) p432-33

7 ibid, p433-34

CHAPTER THREE
THE CALM BEFORE THE STORM

IF A Dublin crow was ever to fly directly eastwards and across the Irish Sea, after 250 miles or so it would reach Maltby in South Yorkshire.

Maltby's population today is about 17,000, but in 1861, just as Irish emigration was in full flow, its population was less than 860[1]. This was a gentle increase on the 679 people living there and recorded in Baines Directory of The County of York, written in 1823[2]. It appears while many millions of Irish were desperate to leave behind the famine and exploitation of their homeland, Maltby was not yet their destination of choice.

This was hardly surprising given that Maltby, situated about eight miles from Rotherham, 13 from Sheffield and 47 from York, could offer little in the way of work.

Unlike its bigger and bolder neighbouring towns and cities, the industrial revolution had yet to take hold in this rural backwater.

Maltby was set in a beautiful, lush, green landscape of rolling farm lands, woods, and a craggy out-crop simply known as "The Crags", where the beck below, with its overhanging shrubs and undergrowth, slowly meandered in sweeping curves through green sloping meadows to the beautiful but tragic atmospheric ruins of the former Cistercian monastery of Roche Abbey.

In the late 19th century, before the mine was opened, the medieval village and the abbey were popular tourist destinations, attracting visitors from the surrounding conurbations on day trips and weekend breaks as they sought moments of light relief from the daily grind in the factories and mills.

The following noteworthy paragraphs are brief descriptions of Maltby and Roche Abbey by a couple of American ladies who visited the area in the early part of the 20th century[3].

In a letter home to her family, Marion Davenport Maltbie wrote: "How I wish you might have been with me this summer while I spent five glorious days in the charming little English village which bears my name. They call it in Yorkshire 'The Queen of Villages'. It deserves the title! So quaint and interesting, preserving all the characteristics of a typical old time village.

"Just a few months later, another American visitor, Neavando A Eldvado also wrote home to her relatives in America, describing Maltby as "the prettiest old village of all".

"But as interested as I was in Maltby, we tore ourselves away, to drive-on a mile further to Roche Abbey," she wrote. "A steep winding road leads down into the valley in which stands the ruins of Roche Abbey. This is the most beautiful spot in all England. It simply beggars description. Such a vale with rocky, shaded fern-covered banks, and broad green pastures: such myriads of wild flowers, bracken, springs, and waterfalls. Shade and sunlight and in the midst of it all stands those grand grey ruins.

"But beneath the beautiful, gentle farmlands of rural South Yorkshire and only a few hundred yards under the soil where Marion and Neavando had both strolled so peacefully, something was stirring.

A huge, dormant volcano was ready to erupt and give up its vast riches, but in the form of coal rather than molten lava.

Prior to the 1900s, due to problems with methane gas, heat and ventilation, this coal had proved difficult to extract. However, with the advent of new mining techniques and the improved steam winding engine and pumps, by the turn of the century this rich coal field, stretching from Leeds in the north, to the Vale of York in the east, to Barnsley in the west and to Nottingham in the south, was ripe for exploitation by the capitalist mining companies and landowners. Marion and Neavando's rural idyll was on the cusp of a revolution.

1   Rotherhamweb.Co.Uk,   *http://www.Rotherhamweb.Co.Uk/district/maltby.Htm*

2 ibid

3 ibid, *http://www.Rotherhamweb.Co.Uk/district/maltbyvisits.Htm*

CHAPTER FOUR
THE YORKSHIRE KLONDIKE

THE letters home by Maltby's American visitors paint a picture of a picture-postcard, sleepy village, its inhabitants gloriously ignorant as to the riches lying in wait under their feet.

However, Marion at least had seen change was coming. She also wrote: "It's a shame but the love of money is the root of all evil. Two railroads are near to Maltby now. One station two miles away and another a mile and a half away. No passengers yet but there will be in time.

"Now they are mining coal on Lord Scarborough's estate and speculators plan to remodel the cunning place. If any of the family want to see our quaint little town still unspoiled let them hurry over to England, for in a year or two many changes are going to take place there and much of the charm will be gone."[1]

Change was definitely coming but it is doubtful even Marion, for all her prescient insight, could quite have predicated the scale of the transformation that was about to unfold.

The following is a newspaper article printed in about 1905, headlined Maltby Main Colliery Company Limited:

"This company has been formed, with a capitol of £350,000 divided into 350,00 shares of £1 pound each, for the purpose of acquiring and working the Barnsley seam of coal under lands near Maltby. 200,000 shares have been applied for by and allotted to the Sheepbridge Coal & Iron Company Limited, and they have already paid the sum of 2s 6d per share thereon. The Sheffield Banking Company Limited, George Street Sheffield, and their branch banks, have this week been authorised to receive applications at par for the remaining 150,000 shares of £1 each, payable as follows: – 1s per share on application, 1s 6d per share on allotment. It is not intended to make any calls for 12 months after allotment, and the remaining 17s 6d per share will probably be called up at intervals during

the following three or four years. Leases from the Earle of Scarborough and others of the said seam under 6,037 acres, or thereabouts, have been obtained and the freehold under 31 acres or thereabouts has been purchased. The Sheepbridge Company have assigned the leases and conveyed the freehold portion to the company in consideration of the sum of £18,804 10s, which has been paid by the company to the Sheepbridge Company. It is anticipated that the Barnsley seam will be found at a depth of from 750 to 800 yards, that it will prove to be from five to six feet thick, and that the quality will be equal to that of adjoining collieries. It is proposed to sink the pits and equip the colliery when necessary with plant capable of raising ultimately from 4,000 to 5,000 tons of coal per day. A railway is being constructed by the South Yorkshire Joint Line Committee from Dinington to Thorn, being an extension of the Shireoaks and Laughton Railway, belonging to the Great Central and Midlands Joint Committee which passes within half a-mile of the proposed site of the pits."[2]

In 1905, shaft sinking contractors for the Chesterfield-based Sheepbridge Coal & Iron Company commenced the sinking of twin mine shafts in a dense woodland clearing to the east of picturesque Maltby, in order to reach the Barnsley Seam. The Barnsley Seam was in fact a 60ins-thick, high-grade coal seam stretching from Barnsley in the west to Maltby in the east.

The motley crew of itinerant shaft sinkers who arrived in Maltby to carry out the job were a special breed of men indeed. They were men of great skills and daring, who rode into the new mine camp with their tents, tools, wooden huts, cranes, pumps, and steam hoists. One witness described them, as like a "tribe of flat capped nomadic warriors". The sinkers arrived aboard rail wagons of the Yorkshire Light Railroad, which was a temporary narrow gauge rail facility to assist the building of Maltby's new mine. As the work advanced, the men, like birds in a nest, rode precariously up and down the shaft in a huge bucket they called the kibble or hoppit. The kibble was suspended by a steel hook and wire line which was attached to the temporary, timber mine-head-frame, which could haul two tons of muck to the surface at one lift, being powered by a steam-winding engine.

Maltby Main Colliery Company Limited, circa 1909

The report to March 31, 1909, states that since March 31, 1908, 1,240 shares have been allotted, bringing up the total to 290,868. The first and second calls have been paid, and notices for the third call, making 10s per shares, have been issued. Sinking operations have been proceeding satisfactorily, the strata passed through consisting principally of rock. No 1 pit has reached a depth of 201 yards and no 2 pit 390 yards. The erection of the permanent plant has made good progress. Six boilers, chimney, electric generator and electric pumps have been completed, and steel headgear and no 2 winding engine are in process of erection. "[3]

Due to the unavailability of records of the precise method of shaft sinking at Maltby Main, the following, in layman's term, is the most likely method to have been used due to the high water content of the formation.

The circular shafts at the early stages would have been dug by pick and shovel then lined with sectional interlocking cast iron tubbing and cast concrete segments as the work progressed. When the water table was reached, the outside perimeter of the shaft would have then been drilled with a series of bore-holes past the water table. A mixture of liquid cement and calcium chloride (salt) would then have been pumped at high pressure into the porous formation, which quickly became solidified. The method allowed the sinker to insert tubbing and continue drilling, blasting, and removing the waste.

Albert Francois, a Belgium engineer, working in the Doncaster area, was the founder of the world-famous Cementation Company Limited. It carried out its first successful contract at Thorn Colliery Yorkshire, in 1910. This was followed by the successful sinking at Hatfield Colliery also in Yorkshire, using its patented liquid cement process, allowing the shafts to be sunk at a rate of 60ft to 80ft per month.

An alternative method, which was used for the first time in Britain in 1909 at Astley Colliery, in Lancashire, was called the "drop shaft", which involved forcing tubbing into the formation by the use of hydraulic jacks allowing the sinkers to excavate. The next section of tubbing was then attached and the process was repeated.

Thyssen Schachtbau, the specialist shaft sinking company from Germany, founded in 1871, developed a similar method to the Cementation Company.

This technique also entailed drilling bore holes around the perimeter of the shaft to reach the water table, followed by freezing the area by means of a freezer unit. After the drilling operation, calcium chloride was then pumped through the freezer unit into the bore-holes, thus freezing the formation and allowing the sinkers to drill, blast, and line the shaft under reasonable conditions. This method was used at the Boulby (Whitby) Potash Mine in the late 1960s. The drilling operation was carried out by German company Deutag Drilling Contractors of Bad Bentheim, whom I had the pleasure of working for for several years in the UK, Germany and the Netherlands.

However, Thyssen's freezing technique was first developed in 1905 and was not used outside Germany until 1911 when it was successfully used in Belgium, dispelling the belief that Thyssen assisted in the shaft sinking at Maltby Main.

As the work underground progressed, back at the surface things were rapidly changing too. The previously idyllic woodland was starting to resemble a makeshift "wild west" mining camp as a conglomeration of offices, timber and tin-shacks, a tin school, workshops and a blacksmith's all took up residency.

Dominating the skyline was the temporary, timber mine-head gear, haulage cranes and tripods, which bellowed steam smoke and ash from this wooded enclave huddled around the two mine shafts and surrounded by a 6ft-high corrugated steel fence. Occasionally, as the shafts deepened, word went round that the sinkers had struck narrow seams of coal, which was a signal for the inhabitants of the camp to raid the shafts' spoil-tip during the night to fill up their coal houses with free, best-quality coal.

This image of a ramshackle "wild west" town taking root in a rural backwater in the heart of Yorkshire was captured by an old time resident Harold Feltrup, who worked at the mine until his retirement. He wrote: "Being told at the age of nine we were going to leave our home in Sheffield and were going to live in the middle of dense woodland in a corrugated tin hut and go to a tin school, I felt I was listening to something out of this world. My father came to the mine in 1908 to work as a blacksmith. The rest of the family came in 1909 to live in the mine camp. I started school in 1909. At that time there were 30 to 35 scholars and two teachers. It was known as the pit school. Later on, as the new village of Maltby began to grow, despite having two extra teachers at the tin school, there were 500 ragged miners children under the age of eleven running wild in the woods and on the crags.

"We had a shop in the camp but it only sold Wild Woodbines (cheap cigarettes) and sweets. When I wasn't going to school it was my job to walk to the village to get more supplies of Woodbines, and I would buy 50 packets of five, then walk all the way back, which was a fair stretch for a small lad".[4]

The sinkers worked 12-hour shifts, seven days a week in the highly dangerous job of getting muck stone and slurry out of the ever deepening holes for weeks on end without missing a shift. Many of the shaft-sinkers were Irish and fleeing the poverty of their homeland in search of a better life.

They included the young Claremorris County Mayo man Bill Connolly, who in later years described the shaft sinkers' life as nothing but "carousing and canoodling", and not far removed from the old gold rush towns of the USA. Bill[5] remarked "the local women would often come out to the mine camp on pay-day holding up their clean aprons for the men to throw in their gold sovereigns".

For all "the carousing and canoodling", shaft-sinking was a desperate job. As a result and often without warning, the urge would come over the men and they'd down tools, head off on the tear and all hell would break loose. On such occasions, much beer and blood was spilt in equal measures between the sinkers and the railroad navies, who were cutting a new railtrack to the new mine site.

In 1909, in conjunction with the mine's construction, hoards of tramp navvies from almost every county in Britain, and many Irish among them, began drifting into the area like an invading army, a reminder of Glenties' county Donegal navvy author and poet Patrick MacGill's fictional characters of the same period; Dermot Flynn, Moleskin Joe and Carroty Dan.

The navvies began forging a branch rail line from the recently opened neighbouring colliery of Dinnington, to the mine site at Maltby, some seven miles in distance. Before the line could be brought to the mine, engineers estimated that a total of 216,000 tons of magnesium limestone shale had to be dug out the ground, which during the winter months was reduced to a quagmire of squelching top-soil and white limestone slurry. Embankments and cuttings of 20ft to 30ft in height and depth were encountered. Muck was shifted by new, American-built mechanical diggers , nicknamed the steam navvy, horse and tipper-cart, and human barrow-runs[6], complemented by picks, shovels, dynamite, blood and sweat[7].

The following passage is from Fred Kitchen's book, Brother To The Ox, first published by his family in the 1940s, ten years after his death[8]. Fred, a local man born and bred, spent most of his life working as a ploughman and wagoner and tied farm labourer during the late 19th and early 20th century, save for a brief spell on the new rail road and a short stint at the new mine. The jobs were Fred's attempts to improve his wages and cast off the yoke of serfdom, which the majority of farm labourers at the time were subjected to under local farmers and landowners.

Fred's dream was to own his own farm, a dream which, sadly, he was never to realise.

Fred, described the tramp navvies, as "a strange nomadic race who just came and went, hundreds of them, where to, and were from, nobody knew or cared. They were a breed the hamlet of Maltby had not seen the likes of before. Much beer and blood began to flow on the streets on Saturday and Sundays. Drunken brawls, revelling, reviling drink-sodden navvies sprawling in the gutter. Many of the navvies camped on Maltby commons, in tents and in rough tin and brattice-cloth shanties[9], anything rather than pay for digs as this would have meant less beer, and more work.

"In that motley crew I witnessed men of education lost to the world in filth and rags, whom drink and misfortune had robbed them of their self respect. Never since the time of the Danes had our little village suffered such an invasion. They were not all heavy drinkers. A lot were steady men who obtained digs with grateful local families. Many of the navvies stayed on in the village when the mine began producing coal". Another witness, the Rev Barrett, of the railway mission, described similar navvies' shacks as "four walls of turf, made by piling sods of earth on top of one another up to a height of six feet and stretching across the top were sagging roof timbers".

All these huts needed, he said, "was the hills of Connemara in the background and Paddy and his pig at the door to make the scene complete"[10].

Fred, who was employed as a nipper for a short period on the new rail construction, described a gang of navvies resting on their haunches in a circle at breakfast time, dressed in traditional navvy attire of boots, moleskin trousers, and green, mother of pearl-buttoned waistcoats. He was surprised to see a man in their midst wearing black garments and a black straw hat, reading from the bible. It was, in fact, the navvy missioner. After his sermon he asked Fred: "And what county tramp are you, young man?".

The following verse from Patrick MacGill's Gleanings From A Navvy's Scrapbook, published in 1910, portrays something of the navvies' lot:

Played Out

As a bullock falls in the crooked ruts,
He fell when the day was o'er,
The hunger gripping his stinted guts,
His body shaken and sore.

They pulled him out of the ditch in the dark,
As a brute is pulled from its lair,
The corps of a navvy stiff and stark,
With the clay on its face and hair...

The navvy's life was tough and often short in the early 20th century, and the remnants of the Truck system or Tommy Shop still prevailed to add to their misery. The system worked by the fact the men were conveniently paid - conveniently for the contractors - on a monthly basis.

More often than not, this meant they were broke and didn't have the money to tie themselves over until the end of the month.

As a result they were forced to sub their wages to the value of the money they had earned. The sub was given in the form of vouchers and could only be exchanged for goods at the "Truck Shop", which was owned and run by the contractor.

Men were diddled wholesale. The goods offered were generally bad; rancid butter and bacon, stale bread, watered down milk, beer and spirits. Prices were higher, and short weight was often given, and on top of that the contractor charged commission of up to ten per cent. But the men had no choice; redeem the tickets at the Truck Shop or starve. When the end of the month came and the value of the tickets they'd subbed were taken away from their wages they were often left with nothing, and so the vicious circle continued. Often unscrupulous contractors were said to make more profit from the Truck Shop than they did from the rail or canal contract itself.

In June of 1910, after four years of back-breaking work by the sinkers under some of the most abominable and dangerous conditions imaginable, oft-times working in oilskins and sou'westers as a result of water seepage from the shafts geological formation, the menacing twin black holes were completed to a depth of 818 yards each (2,454ft , by 20ft in diameter), with only one death being recorded. Maltby Main Colliery Company Limited, circa 1911

"The annual report of the directors of the Maltby Main Colliery Company limited for the year to March 31, 1911, states that the Barnsley seam was reached at a depth of 818yards in the no2 pit in June last year, and in the no1 pit in January last. The operation of heading out through the shaft pillar and the equipment of the shafts have since been vigorously prosecuted. Coal is now being raised, and the output will in a short time increase at a rapid rate. The total thickness of the coal is 7ft 4ins, about 5ft 2in. of which may be regarded as workable. The quality of both the hards and softs is excellent, and so far as it as it as already been tested in the market, has given satisfaction to the buyers. The equipment of no2 shaft, together with the first installment of the screens and sidings, capable of dealing with 2,500 tons of coal per day, has been completed, and the preparation of no1 pit and its winding engines is being rapidly carried on. Eight boilers have been erected and fitted with automatic stokers and slack delivery apparatus, and two more are being fixed. The power plant consisting of 250kw, high-pressure steam generators, together with ventilating fan and

engines, lamp room and workshops have been completed. One hundred and thirty six workmen's houses have been erected, and it is intended to build 128 more this year." [11]

The gold rush for Maltby's black diamonds was on! Hundreds of mine-head erectors, tunnel miners, construction workers, and engineers, descended on the mine campsite from all points of the compass to ready the mine for producing coal.

In June of the same year, a huge dinner party was held, hosted by the mining company to celebrate reaching the mother load. Among the many distinguished guests was Lord Scarborough (no connection with the coastal town), of Sandbeck Park Estate, and his Lumley family entourage, whose vast swathes of lands lay above the rich seams. A 60-year agreement was reached with Lord Scarborough and Maltby Colliery Company Limited to extract coal from underneath his land. In 1907, the first entry of rent paid by the mining company for Maltby to the Sandbeck Estate was reputedly £2,850 - £273,859 in today's money.

The estate continued to extract rent from the mine until I left the area in the 1960s. The Earl of Scarborough was one of the richest men in the UK.

But our area of South Yorkshire was not alone in this great metaphorical gold rush, as countless shafts were being sunk the length and breadth of this vast new deep-mine coalfield. Mine head-frames were as numerous as village church spires. Never before had the region seen such a movement of men, machinery, and equipment as thousands of workers and their families descended in biblical proportions on the mines and villages like transient moles throughout this enormous Yorkshire Klondike.

1 Rotherhamweb.Co.Uk, *http://www.Rotherhamweb.Co.Uk/district/maltbyvisits.Htm*
2 Colliery Guardian Newspaper, North of England Institute Of Mining And Mechanical Engineers
3 ibid
4 Clifford Auckland, The Growth Of A Township: Maltby's Story, Rotherham Metropolitan Borough Council Libraries, Museum & Arts

Department (1989)

5 Although it was said Bill Connolly was unable to read or write, his skills with maths and measurements in the shafts and headings made him an invaluable member of the shaft-sinking crew. Young Bill married Ann Filburn, the daughter of Scotsman Rocky Filburn, the foreman shaft-sinker at Maltby, while living on the camp. Later their first son, Harry, was born in a tin house on the site. After the mine went into production, a number of Irish sinkers stayed on in Maltby to work at the pit, and were given company houses in the same street, Schofield Crescent, which became known as Sinkers' Row.

6 Barrow run; wooden planking was spaced at intervals up the side of the cutting enabling barrow and man to be pulled up the side of the cutting by means of a horse, rope and pulley block stationed at the top of the bank.

7 The vast rail network under construction to the mines eventually served Sheffield's steel making plants, the north of England, the Midlands' manufacturing industries and the domestic coal markets of the capital. The rail network also had links to Yorkshire's extensive canal system, connecting not only the Aire and Calderdale mainline with Sheffield and South Yorkshire but also Sheffield with the river Trent via the Sheffield and South Yorkshire navigation system which was built in 1891 to increase the scope of the coal trade. Work started in 1896 and it was opened in 1905. The system also had links to terminals on the river Humber and to the ports of Hull, Goole, and Grimsby, and beyond to worldwide markets.

8 Fred Kitchen, Brother To The Ox, Caliban Books (1982)

9 A partition used in a coal mine and made from heavy, waterproof cotton. They were often stolen and used on miners' sheds.

10 Daniel William Barrett, Life And Work Among The Navvies, (2008 new ed) Biblio Bazaar

11 Colliery Guardian Newspaper loc. cit.

CHAPTER FIVE
BUILDING A COMMUNITY

MINERS, just like moles, need somewhere to rest after a long day tunnelling and by 1911, when Maltby Main Colliery was officially opened, the ancient village had already lost much of its rural nature. Hundreds of miners and their families had arrived from mining communities scattered throughout the United Kingdom, often via the newly built Maltby Railway Station, which was situated adjacent to the mine, and was opened in 1910 by the South Yorkshire Joint Railway Company[1].

In 1909, the colliery company had begun building row upon row of colliery cottages to cater for the large influx of mine workers and their families.

It was named, somewhat bizarrely because it sounds more like a tourist destination of miniature homes in a fanciful setting than a place tough-as-teak miners would raise their families and forge a community, Maltby Model Village.

"Model" was used in the sense of an ideal to which other developments could aspire and Maltby Model Village was just one of many number of such communities built from the late 18th century onwards by industrialists to house their workers.

Although the villages were located close to industrial sites, they were generally physically separated from them and often consisted of relatively high-quality housing, with integrated community amenities and attractive physical environments. The design of Maltby's new village was presumably based on the world famous model village of Saltaire, built in the countryside, three miles from Bradford in West Yorkshire.

Its beautifully designed, cut-stone dwellings were built in the 1850s by the philanthropic woollen mill owner Sir Titus Salt to house his workers and their families.

His village was remarkable in its day, and contained bathhouses, a hospital, an institute for recreation and education, almshouses, allotments, a school, a park, concert hall, gymnasium, library and churches.

Sir Titus had perhaps hit upon the still relatively new idea, first sparked in 1786 by David Dale, the founder of the cotton mill village of New Lanark in Scotland, that a happy, well-housed, well-fed work force, would be more productive.

Maltby's Model Village eventually contained more than 1,000 homes, of two and three bedrooms for the workers, and four-bedroomed houses for the overmen (shift supervisors) and deputies. The façade of the homes was a sombre, dark-red brickwork, some with cement stucco, giving the effect that the dwellings had been there forever.

The layout of the village was the brainchild of architects Messrs Fredrick Hopkinson & Co, of Nottinghamshire, who, it appears, were given a free hand to design the villages throughout the coalfield. The layout was one of concentric circles containing an Anglican Church, a school, a miners' institute, The Lido (a swimming pool) a huge sports field, a beautiful Victorian-period bandstand and the infamous Queen's Hotel, all company owned.

The model houses at Maltby, said Lord Scarborough at a miners' Anglican Church garden fete[2], were an attempt by the mining company to avoid the "squalor and misery" which was a well-known but sad feature of older mining communities. Model villages such as at Maltby were certainly in sharp contrast to the slums that had developed in English towns and cities over much of the century, which were characterised by dark, overcrowded and insanitary housing, with everything covered by filth and soot from the neighbouring chimneys of factories and houses.

However, despite Lord Scarborough's claims that the building of such model villages were a genuine attempt to lift workers out of a life of squalor and misery, I believe the building of colliery houses and leisure facilities by the mining companies were not necessarily just an act of convenience or benevolence, but were arguably a means of social control too.

On many occasions in the past this strategy had been used against miners during disputes and strikes.

An example was that of Maltby's neighbouring mining community of Denaby Main. The despotic Denaby & Cadeby Colliery Company had used the threat of eviction on several separate occasions during disputes.

It was in 1902/3, during what was termed the Bag Muck Strike[3], that the company evicted the miners and their families from their homes. As result, miners were forced to seek shelter in tents on a nearby craggy outcrop, in disused barns and chapels and in a local wooded area during the harsh winter of 1902.

The following is a transcript from an article which appeared in a local newspaper of January 1903:

"By Friday, January 9, the evictions at Denaby Main were completed. No riots had taken place and relations between the police and strikers were amicable. The show of force, with some of the police being armed with cutlasses, may have had some influence, but the general feeling seemed to be that the police themselves did not relish their task ahead and tried to carry out their duty with as much thought and co-operation as was possible.

"Snow fell during that January week, and the evicted families, housed in chapels and under canvas, could not have had an easy time. In one instance, a tent was expected to provide accommodation for 60 men. Since the school in Denaby Main was owned by the company, no strikers were housed there and there is nothing in the local press at the time which suggests that accommodation was made available at the parish church of All Saints' Denaby Main, which had also been built by the company. The Roman Catholic Church of Saint Alban's and the Wesleyan Methodist Chapel are also conspicuous by their absence from the mentioned list of accommodation. The foremost providers of shelter for the evicted miners and their families were in fact the Primitive Methodists in Denaby Mexborough and Goldthorp, and the Baptist Church at Denaby Main. The parish church at Mexborough did, however, provide a barn, whilst Mexborough UDC made a schoolroom and the empty smallpox hospital available. In addition, a general committee of miners from other collieries helped to make arrangements for tent accommodation for those unable to find other shelter."

Whatever the reasoning for the building of Maltby Model Village, be it a genuine attempt by the mine owners to build a utopian community offering comfortable homes and plenty of leisure facilities or merely a means of extending their control over an already subservient workforce, you didn't have to scratch much below the surface to find life behind the new brickwork had changed little.

An article published in the missionary publication The Christian Budget of 1899 about the problems encountered by the writer at Denaby, less than ten miles from Maltby, could well have been true of any mining settlement where an itinerant workforce was employed.

The article was titled: The Worst Village In England.

> *"I am sitting down to write this article in numb despair, for the community I have to describe is so repulsive that many who have never been near it will refuse to credit the story.*
>
> *"Denaby Main ought to be paradise. Every man there has ample work, wages are very high and each family can have a house to itself for very low rent. The eight-hour day has been granted, the country around ranks among the most beautiful in the country. In Denaby Main no adult need be hungry or ill clad save through deliberate choice. It ought to be an ideal community, but instead it is almost hell on earth.... The gambling craze has seized hold on it. With gambling comes a long train of other evils, until today the name of the place is passing into a by-word. The whole of the land is divided between two proprietors:- the colliery company is the largest owner and exercisers practically despotic powers in the village, and owns all the houses, having specially erected them for its men. There is street after street of little two storied dwellings evidently put up in very cheap style. The miners are charged between four and five shillings per week (as a rule) for these and their rent is stopped from their wages, but the men have little to complain about in the matter of wages, an expert miner can easily earn his seven to eight shillings a day. Yet not withstanding this high wage a very large proportion of the families have not a penny left on Monday morning. The regular method of living in Denaby is to pay debts on Saturday and get things out of*

pawn, spend all the remainder of their wages on Saturday night and Sunday, and start pawning on Monday morning again. On Saturday afternoon and evening in particular, the place is like a pandemonium when the men play pitch and toss.

"The first rush on Saturday night is to the public house. The colliery company with a philanthropy worthy of praise has resolved that the poor fellows shall not have far to go for a drink, it has built a great public house of its own, the profits of this place must be enormous. The house is full continually and on Saturday and Sunday, the scenes that go round it are amazing in their grotesque horror. An old Irishman who lived in the neighbourhood once well summed up the situation. He was so troublesome on Saturday night that the police had to take charge of him. Then, going along with the police, he turned reflective. 'This is a funny place', he said. 'First we go to the office to get our wages, then the company builds us a place where we can give the money back to it, and then when the money has gone it provides you to take care of us'.

"Half of the women in Denaby are fierce and persistent gamblers. Towards the end of the week some of the houses are stripped of almost everything on which money can be raised. 'What's the use of trying to stop?', the women cry if you talk to them. 'If we don't do it the men will. We might as well spend the money as anybody else. A short life and a merry one we say'. The ruin of the children is especially sad. The first thing that struck me when walking down the main street of Denaby was the large number of children with sore eyes. I saw more ophthalmic girls in the street in 20 minutes than I see in the slums of London in 20 days. 'It's the dirt that does it', said one man. 'Our women folk are too busy with the bookmakers to care for their bairns.'" "The proportion of ragged children amazed me when I remember that all their parents were earning high wages. The moral nature of the children is warped in some cases. There are some families in Denaby with incomes of about three pounds a week where the only furniture in the living room is a box and a table, the box serving as a chair."[4]

The erecting of a bandstand in Maltby Model Village underlined, in my eyes at least, just how far removed the idealism of the mine owners and their architects was from the reality of the daily grind of their workers. The bandstand was seemingly bestowed upon a huddled Edwardian mass, tugging their forelocks in deference at the munificence of their bosses and so perpetuating an image of a well-ordered, well-mannered, cultured community.

But it was just that – an image, a façade. Certainly, in my time living in Maltby, I cannot recall the bandstand ever being used. The idea of miners promenading the village with their families in their Sunday finery while the Maltby Concert Brass Band played on was just a pipe dream. Miners, momentarily free from the grind and dangers of the pitface, had more pressing matters to attend to, which was consuming as much "Amber Nectar" as they could before the cry of "last orders".

Miners worldwide have a reputation for drink and the miners of Maltby were no exception. They had a tremendous capacity and a reputation for beer, although many would claim it was for "medicinal purposes". Indeed, anyone in the village would tell you that a miner needed beer to replace lost fluids due to the 100 degree temperatures he worked in underground. It appeared, though, that it was a vicious circle, because the harder you worked the more you had to drink. It was said the mineworkers who didn't drink were not particularly good workers.

Twenty pints or more wouldn't be an over exaggeration for a Saturday or Sunday afternoon or evening session. It was no big deal for a miner and his mates coming off the afternoon shift to call at The Queen's Hotel for the last hour when they would knock back ten pints each and walk home with not a bother on them. All traces of alcohol would soon disappear from their system.

The Queen's Hotel, the infamous miners' pub in the heart of the Maltby, was a company pub, built and run by the mining company - what they gave with one hand it took back with the other - and was out of all proportion to the size of the village. The Queen's boasted a huge concert room complete with a theatre-style stage. Often, old vaudeville-type acts and Can-Can dancing girls performed at weekends to a packed house and the delight of exclusively mining men. The Queen's also sported a tap room, smoke room, snug and off-licence, where I used to go to take empty pint bottles for Blanch, the barmaid, to fill-up from the pump's for my dad. His thirst quencher after he came home from an afternoon shift was best bitter. Another section of the pub also housed a knitwear factory, where many of the local girls worked making stockings. The Queen's also had a stylish lounge bar too, which could be said was an oasis of respectability and was the domain of Maltby's mostly respectable, clannish Irish miners. This they frequented early on a Saturday and Sunday evening before leaving to meet their wives at the Catholic Club, where they could always be seen in their smart Sunday-best attire of blue or brown suits, white shirt and tie, flat caps or felt Trilby hats.

When I was a lad, fights and drunkenness were commonplace inside and outside this Wild West saloon. It wasn't unusual to see a miner crouching under a table re-enacting with imaginary pick and shovel how he'd worked in a low coal seam the previous week.

A sad reflection of the times was to see some poor, unfortunate badly-dressed downtrodden miner's wife, patiently waiting outside for the remains of her husband's wages.

On Sunday mornings, on our way back from Mass, we could witness scores of the roughest singlet-clad miners patiently squatting on their haunches at the kerbside waiting for midday opening time. As we passed-by, my mother would look down scornfully on them.

The demon drink always had its downside and was the cause of much fighting, feuds, family rows and poverty. However, it also offered miners the chance to relax, socialise and blow off steam and whenever they overstepped the mark the local bobby, PC Lambton, was always there to cart them off.

Even in my day, miners had the reputation of being extremely primitive and unsophisticated and were, on the whole, denigrated by the rest of society.

The building of a bandstand was never likely to alter such opinions and, in truth, the behavior of some of the miners merely played into the hands of their detractors. I recall one female resident of Maltby keeping a horse in her scullery until the county health department paid her a visit.

Pigeons, hens, ducks, geese, greyhounds, whippets and ferrets were all part of the rich tapestry of many a miner's backyard and garden. Cats and dogs roamed at will, as did children, in overgrown garden-jungles and patches of unkempt land, which no one seemed to have the will or notion to keep tidy. The illegal bookies was often a pleasurable pastime for many miners, my dad being no exception when he placed his bet with Connie Marshall, the "clerk" at the bookies hut on Saturday afternoons on the spare piece of land at the back of Salisbury Road.

Greyhound and whippet racing was another popular miner's pastime (even the parish priest, Father Mullan, was reputed to have bred and raced greyhounds from his kennels at nearby Hellaby).

Training greyhounds required an upturned bicycle with a fixed gear, a 200-yard length of fine line attached to a wide-rimmed back wheel minus its tyre and a piece of rabbit fur. Great speeds could be obtained as the operator furiously wound the pedals by hand on the Silver Dollar fields with the greyhound in hot pursuit of the rabbit fur.

They were an incorrigible lot. However, despite their faults, miners and their families on the whole were an extremely generous, genuine, and friendly breed, although very clannish by nature of the isolated villages the mines were situated in. Many outsiders, especially Rotherham folk, feared mining villages like the plague, and those well-to-do residents who were caught up in the building of new mining settlements soon fled the area.

One writer referred to pit men and their families as "the tribe". However, my dad often commented on the loyalty and comradeship of all miners above and below ground as a thing to behold, which couldn't be found in any other walk of life.

This very real sense of community and comradeship was all the more remarkable because Maltby, thanks largely to the very transient nature of the mining industry, was a melting pot of cultures and accents.

Visitors to the area would have noted accents from Durham, Wales Lancashire, Derbyshire, Leicestershire, Staffordshire, West Yorkshire and, of course, the west of Ireland, down the pit and on the streets. The late Clifford Auckland, the Anglican minister at Maltby, interestingly portrayed the development of Maltby in his short manuscript, The Growth Of A Township: Maltby's Story, published in 1989.

For reasons known only to himself, the Rev Auckland excluded a most important section of the community, that being the Irish. As a result, the Irish community was effectively written out of Maltby's history, and to an extent this error is still perpetuated today. "What did the Irish do for Maltby?" one member of a local history society once told – she wasn't really asking - me.

But to ignore the Irish contribution to Maltby is much more than a mistake. It's a blunder of epic proportions for they played a crucial role in its development, its religious life and its future prosperity.

Irish shaft-sinkers had played a significant role in the sinking of the mine-shafts and then in 1911 when the mine began producing coal, they came to the village in significant numbers to work in the pit. They soon became the most organised group in the village and together with their children, their teachers and parish priest made remarkable efforts to belie the stereotypical images so often bestowed upon them.

Initially, the steady influx of first, second and third generation Irish Catholic miners and their families relocating to the village needed somewhere to address their spiritual needs.

Being without a place of worship, to begin with masses were held in an upstairs room on occasional Sundays at the local White Swan Inn (who's owners were the aptly named Bishop family), situated in the old village of Maltby. A visiting priest from the neighbouring parish of Oldcoats, some seven miles from Maltby, would attend to say Mass. In 1912, the village on behalf of the Catholic population was conferred the status of a mission by the diocese of Leeds.

Yorkshire-man Father Thomas Parkin, born in 1843 and ordained at Ushaw in 1868, was appointed the first parish priest. The parish comprised Maltby, and Dinnington. In 1913, Dinnington became a separate parish and father Parkin remained as parish priest of Maltby. The first temporary church was opened on January 18, 1914. The prefabricated building was brought to the village and erected on a site adjoining the model village.

It would be reasonable to say, going by its aged-looks when I was growing up, that the church had already done the rounds as a temporary place of worship serving the many older mining parishes. Not on record is the purchase of land for the church, although the funds are thought to have been raised by Catholic miners and purchased from the Maltby Colliery Company. In the same year, in an endeavour to cater for the miners' huge thirst and social needs, Maltby Catholic Club [Irish Club] was also founded.

Again due to a lack of any tangible records, it can only be assumed the purchase of the land was made possible by the generosity of the miners themselvesThe Irish of this new village had built their own church, school and social club, and some branched out with their own businesses.

They were extremely hard working and respectable. As is the case with most immigrants, they had a strong desire to better themselves, which in Maltby they did to good effect.

1 Two years later on October 3, 1912, Rotherham Corporation Transport took advantage of the large number of building workers employed building the Model Village by launching its first trolley bus service to Maltby. The first route began at the terminus at Herringthorpe on the outskirts of the town and called at Wickersley and Bramley terminating in Maltby where the Queen's Hotel now stands.

2 Clifford Auckland, loc cit.

3 In layman's terms, it was brought about as a result of coalface workers having to dig away the bag muck, which was a seam of muck stone and dross, preventing the miners getting at the coalface. The miners were paid by the ton for getting coal only – meaning the bag muck had to be cleared first before workers could be paid. As time went by, the bag muck seam became increasingly thicker, which meant the miners were spending more of their time shifting the bag muck, resulting in a serious reduction of their already meagre wages

4 Conisbrough & Denaby Main Local History *https://sites.Google.Com/ site/conisbroughlocalhistory/home*

CHAPTER SIX
DEATH AND DISASTER

THE sometimes merciless behaviour of their bosses as witnessed during the Bag Muck Strike of 1902/3 and the inhumane working conditions they had to endure were not the only challenges facing pitmen. Indeed, they were far from the most challenging, for just keeping their wits about them in order to stay alive was a daily battle that every man toiling underground had to bear.

On July 9, 1912, an explosion occurred at the nearby Denaby and Cadeby pit which resulted in the tragic loss of 88 lives, with 54 of the victims coming from the village of Denaby alone.

It was said one of the miners involved in the rescue operation claimed the scene of the disaster was so horrible that he would never go in the mine again. A short time later he reportedly committed suicide by drowning in the nearby River Don, creating yet another victim of the disaster.

Life goes on, as they say, and mining resumed one week later, but the disaster had created 61 widows and left 132 children without fathers. In total, during its 100-year history, 426 men and boys lost their lives at Denaby and Cadeby Colliery.

Indeed, in the period from 1850 to 1950, it is estimated about 145,000 people lost their lives in UK mines[1], an average of 1,450 deaths a year, or almost four deaths a day, making mining arguably the most dangerous job of its time.

Maltby Main was not immune from tragedy. Just like the majority of mines in the deep coalfields, it was in essence a hot and gaseous pit, with pockets of methane gas lurking in its maze of coalseams. The mine, inevitably, experienced its share of disasters, fatalities and gruesome accidents, although one particular incident in 1923 stands out above all others.

Gob fires had been a source of intermittent trouble for several years at the Maltby mine; spontaneous outbreaks of smoldering in the heaps of debris with which the "gob holes" - worked out places in the coal seam - were filled. These gob fires were extremely difficult to quench and were, of course, very dangerous, particularly in mines like that at Maltby, which was home to the 5 foot thick Barnsley Seam. Adding to the problem was the fact Maltby mine was known to be particularly hot with a high methane emission.

It was this highly explosive gas which caused the terrible underground explosion on Saturday, July, 28, 1923, in which 27 men, about one per cent of the entire working population at the colliery, lost their lives. The subsequent report into the tragedy that followed by the Chief Inspector of Mines, Sir Thomas Mottram, traced the events which led to the disaster[2]. Sir Thomas noted a "gob stink", the odour from burning coal given off by an underground fire, was first detected in an airway on April 26. Efforts were made to contain the fire - after all, the life of the pit and indeed the village was threatened - but the problem kept recurring throughout May, June and early July.

On May 17, the manager and an overman were seriously gassed. Despite the best efforts to extinguish or at least contain the fire, it continued to spread and on July 13 there was a major roof collapse, leaving a number of men injured.

The manager ordered the effected area to be flooded but a conference of mining engineers cancelled the order and, as a result, union officials later asked for their members to return to the task of saving the pit. They duly recommenced work on Sunday night, July 22, in preparation for an offensive against the "gob fire" with some 80 men employed on this difficult task.

At a meeting on the following Wednesday, a request was presented to the colliery management for a further 100 men to be used for safety work. The request stated: "If the work proceeded satisfactorily, coal-getting may be resumed within the next fortnight". "Coal getting" was the miners' livelihood and they were ready to risk their lives in order to protect it.

Shortly after 9am on Saturday, July 28, the first report of something untoward happening down below filtered through to the colliery offices almost 1,000 yards above where the miners had been valiantly trying to contain the fire.

The inspector's report reveals just what had happened.

It states: "On the morning of July 28, 1923, a new shift of men, numbering 122 in addition to officials, descended the pit at about

6am. While work was proceeding on the 'stoppage' a violent explosion occurred. The explosion not only killed 27 unfortunate men, but so blocked the underground approach roads so that only one body could be recovered, save that of Original Renshaw.

"The Rotherham Advertiser described the scene at the pithead. Its journalist wrote: "There came what was a death blow to all hope.

"There are various eyewitness accounts of that terrible day. One of the most moving is that of Arthur Daniels, who was a young man working in the colliery's offices[3].

He was on duty on the Friday afternoon before the fateful Saturday and his job in the "tally office"[4] gave him a grandstand view of the appalling tragedy as it unfolded. Arthur said: "It was known that the outlook was serious and that there was severe danger of the pit blowing up. A call for volunteers had gone out to seal off the serious 'firedamp' area. Twenty seven men responded including colliery deputies and colliers who knew well the grave dangers."

After the explosion on Saturday morning, Arthur returned to the tally office out of a sense of moral duty and a genuine desire to offer some sort of assistance. He said: "The office was supposed to be closed on Saturdays. In the event, I did the right thing. A director asked me for a list of the entombed men. He asked me to refer all pressmen to the manager's office. "As I approached the pithead for duty I was confronted by a crowd including St John Ambulance ladies, womenfolk and also men from other collieries. It all showed the deep affection and solidarity of the well-trained personnel in mining. Many bitter tears were shed by wives and relatives who mingled in the great crowd.

"Of the 122 men who were underground on that fateful Saturday when the explosion happened, the vast majority were far enough away from the seat of the explosion to be saved. But those who died were 600 yards away from the fire they were fighting.

The fire spread swiftly through the seam and the roadways to annihilate them all. Their heroism and that of the men fortunate enough to survive was indeed a noble effort to save the livelihood of all who lived in the mining village.

Only half an hour after the explosion, the first rescuers entered the cage and went underground. The rescuers included miners and their faithful union leaders Ted Dunn and Hughie Ross. Men from the Rotherham Mine Rescue Station augmented the four Maltby Rescue teams but to no avail. By the evening of the fateful Saturday the rescuers reported that the hope of finding anyone still alive underground was gone.

The mine was closed and Arthur recalled he soon took up the position of secretary of the colliery's football club because John Overman, a colliery official and previous club secretary, had been killed in the explosion.

The funeral of Original Renshaw, the only victim to be recovered from the scene of the disaster, was held at the Church of the Ascension. The Bishop of Sheffield conducted the service. The church was packed to capacity with 500 mourners.

Those attending included government officials, the mine's directors, relatives and general well-wishers and mourners, who were unable to take a seat in the overcrowded church but lined the streets outside to pay their respects.

Among the tragically long list of victims was a young man of 26 who came not from Maltby, but from Darnall, in Sheffield. His name in the list of victims stands out. All the others were mineworkers and mine officials. Edward Clixby was the research chemist at the neighbouring colliery of Dinington. Because Maltby did not have research chemist. Edward was sent to test for the concentration of gas. He went down the shaft that fateful morning and never returned. Miners said his little sports car remained in the pit yard for many weeks; a sad, poignant reminder of the bitter tragedy.

Maltby already had a bleak existence. It now faced a far bleaker future. At first it was thought that the damage was so great the pit would have to be abandoned.

But unemployment pay at the time was only 15 shillings for a man, with an extra five shillings a week for his wife and one shilling for each of their children[5]. Quite simply, the miners and their families could not afford for the pit to close.

Subsequently on August 4, 1923, less than two weeks after the tragedy, work started to make the pit safe by sealing off the damaged area.

Little more than a month later, at midnight on September 8 to be precise, a group of miners went back underground to start the first shift since the explosion that had killed so many of their comrades[6].

Misfortune, death and misery had dogged Maltby Mine for much of its short existence, yet it had survived thanks largely to the sheer doggedness of the miners, their families and mine officials.

Around about the time of the Maltby tragedy, some 400 miles west in Donegal my father was making tentative plans to flee Ireland's great poverty and, like hundreds and thousands of his Irish brethren, start a new life in England. Such was the everyday occurrence of death and disaster in the mines of Britain at that time, it is highly unlikely the news of the tragedy at Maltby would have reached Ireland. Had it done so, maybe, just maybe, it may have forced my father to think again about heading to England in search of a better life. But then again, probably not. Tragedy and heartache had been a regular visitor in my father's relatively short life up to that point, so it was extremely unlikely the deaths of a handful of men in a remote Yorkshire township would have been able to cast serious doubt on his simple aspirations of regular work and a regular wage.

1 The Coalmining History Resource Centre, *www.Cmhrc.Co.Uk* It is possible the death toll in the mines could have been as high as 250,000 with injuries running at 150,000 per year by the time of the First World War. Other mine disasters included the death of 168 miners in 1909 in at West Stanley in County Durham; 136 killed at Wellington in Whitehaven, Cumberland in 1910; 439 killed in 1939 at the Universal Senghenydd pit in Glamorgan.

2 Rotherhamweb.Co.Uk, *http://www.Rotherhamweb.Co.Uk/maltby/index. Htm*

3 Clifford Auckland, loc cit; (Arthur's father had come to Maltby after being appointed professional bandmaster to the new colliery band. After service in the First World War and having tasted action at the Battle of Passchendaele, Arthur got a job in the colliery's offices).

4 Each miner had a numbered disc which was given to him when he descended the pit in the cage. A duplicate with the same number was kept by the "banksman" at the surface. If at the end of a shift one of the miner's tally had not been handed in to the banksman it was known that particularly miner had not returned to the surface.

5 The Ministry of Health refused an application from the Rotherham Board of Guardians for a contribution of £50 towards a relief fund!

6 Those who died were- John Stoker aged 30, overman; George Perrins 37,

deputy; Harry Norwood, 30, deputy; Ernest Clixby, 26, analyst; Richard Ernest Dunn ,28, collier; John Henry Garratty, 38 , corporal; William Emberton, 27, collier. George Hickling, 47, ripper; John William Green, 38, byeworker; Silvanus Turner, 27, collier; George Brierley, 34, collier, William Preece, 24, collier; Aaron Daniels, 46, collier; Bertie Bearshall, 29, collier; Leonard Meredith, 22, collier; Albert Smithson, 28, collier; Joseph Best, 19, filler; Richard John Brooks, 24, collier; Joseph Spibey, 29, collier; John Chandler Spilsbury, 33, collier; Raymond Clinton Bourne, 18, haulage hand; Harold Bourne, 35, haulage hand; Benjamin Jones, 26, collier; Alfred Leslie Fellows, 15 , haulage hand. Original Renshaw, 48, roadlayer; Edward Mitchell, 23, byeworker.

CHAPTER SEVEN
BRED FOR EXPORT

My father, Hugh Fergus Carney (Aodh Fearghus O'Cearnaigh), was born in December 1903, the third son of James and Mary (nee Sweeney) and one of ten children in all.

Mary hailed from the townlands of Drumkeelan, which neighboured with Edrim Glebe in South Donegal.

The population was a mixture of native Catholic Irish, and Ulster Scots Protestants (The Ascendancy[1]) who were descended from the plantation of Ulster from 1610-1630.

Dad attended Glencoagh National School but the boys from the Glebe were a wild bunch, I've often been told, thus the school was in the practice of rounding them up and bringing them to school in a cart, covered with netting.

My grandparents eked out a miserable living as farmers or cottiers in that rough, hilly terrain close to the village of Mountcharles overlooking the beautiful picturesque Donegal Bay and the Blue Stack Mountains in the parish of Killymard, in south–west Donegal. Dad's father, James, the youngest of the male Carneys, was born in 1872 only 22 years after the devastating Great Famine. My great-grandparents, Patrick and Sophia, lived through that tragic period, and it is likely they would have been newly married between the years 1845 and 1850, when huge numbers of tenant farmers in Donegal lost their homes, their farms, their land, and their self respect in order to survive and keep starvation at bay.

As a million people were starving to death, Sir Charles Edward Trevelyan, the British Government's head of famine relief, infamously wrote: "The judgment of God sent the calamity to teach the Irish a lesson, that calamity must not be mitigated. The real evil with which we have to contend with is not the physical evil of the famine, but the moral evil of the selfish perverse and turbulent character of the people."[2]

With such a man seemingly in charge of leading the relief effort in

Ireland, is it any wonder the help forthcoming from the British was to prove so limited and ineffectual?

Many desperate men were put to work on useless public works schemes, an example of which can be found today on any number of roads that lead to no-where in particular.

The women of Killymard - my great-grandmother Sophia being no exception - went out on the highways and byways, to places they would not be recognised, and begged. Many, it was said, would prefer to die from hunger and the cold rather than go begging but the workhouse, a last resort, was the starving populations' greatest fear. Admission meant giving up their land, their homes and livestock in order for their children and themselves to be fed.

With much luck and by the grace of God, Patrick and Sophia survived the famine with their home and land intact[3].

They were, however, to witness over time their children Patrick, John Manus, Hugh, James (my grandfather), Bridget, Winnie, Anne and Kate join the mass emigration to America. (It is certain one child, Susan, remained in Ireland and she later died in a psychiatric hospital in Letterkenny, Donegal, in 1934; there are no records of what happened to another daughter, Unity, other than she was born in 1871, while Margaret, who was born in 1867, died in 1889 aged only 22.).

It must have been a heartbreaking time for my great grandparents, waving goodbye to so many of their children and never really expecting to see them again.

But it was a situation replicated in thousands of homes across Ireland at that time. As the young men and women were forced to flee Irelands shores, it became the custom among the close knit communities of the west, including Donegal, that anyone emigrating to America or Australia would tour the village or country areas for a couple of days before their departure. Dubbed The American Wake, they would visit the house of every friend and neighbour to say goodbye. There would be much sorrow and laments in every house, and blessings galore would be offered to every emigrant.

In the evening, people of the district would gather at the family home where much drinking, music, dancing and song would take place. Food was provided by neighbours; whisky, poitin[4] and tobacco would be plentiful, as would a fiddler or two. At various times in the night, the practice of keening, a form of vocal lament associated with mourning that is traditional in Scotland, Ireland and some African and American cultures, would also be heard.

As dawn approached, the real lamentations would begin. The person starting out on his long and often perilous journey would be soaked with tears and kisses amid wailing and much sorrow. The entire gathering would then accompany the traveller for several miles along the road at the beginning of his journey and then they would mournfully stand until the emigrant was out of sight. As often as not, that would be the last they would see of them.

In 1911, like thousands more of his poverty stricken countrymen, my grandfather, James, leaving behind his wife, Mary, and their young children, including my father, Hugh, upped sticks and, with only $15 in his pocket, left for America in search of a regular wage in order to support his growing brood back in Ireland.

On his arrival on America's east coast, James would have made the six-day journey to join his brother Manus and sisters Annie, Winnie and Kate[5], who had lived in the infamous, Irish-run copper mining town of Butte, Montana, in the American West, since the 1880s.

Dubbed the Richest Hill On Earth, County Cavan man Marcus Daly, who had fled Ireland as a 15-year-old after the Great Famine, is often credited with transforming the fortunes of Butte and its any number of immigrants.

Daly, a former itinerant hard rock miner, eventually became a multi-millionaire, owning land, mines, railroads, smelters and racehorses. By 1900, half of Butte's 30,000 population were said to be Irish, with several thousand working in Daly's mines.

The Irish had got to Butte first, hot on the heels of Daly[6], and as a result the town became the most organised Irish community in the United States.

The Irish ran the unions, the mines, the police force, the fire department, and the education department and Butte had numerous Irish judges and even eight Cork-born mayors.

Two of the Carney brothers, Pat and Hugh, had also made it to Butte but had been killed in the early years of the 20th century before my grandfather, James, had arrived Stateside.

Pat was shot dead in a gunfight in a dispute over wages at the Cora Mine on September 12, 1902.

Hugh, whom my father was named after, was a stationary engineer and union official. He died after falling some 1,600ft from a mine cage as he was descending the Bell Diamond Mine on January 6, 1909.

The eldest Carney brother, John, had also made a life for himself for a time in Butte, but had died of lung disease from the mines' toxic dust shortly after returning to Ballydavitt in Donegal with his West Cork-born wife, Margaret, and their children in 1901.

With James now working alongside his brother and sisters in Butte, back home in Donegal my grandmother, Mary, continued to support herself and her children on a subsistence level with seasonal work, spinning, and the odd remittance from my grandfather in America. Grandfather returned to Donegal in 1914 to prepare to take his family, including my dad who would have been now aged ten or 11, back to Montana to start what he thought would be a new, more prosperous, life for them all.

Big wages were to be earned working underground. Butte miners were the highest paid manual workers in the United States, but then they needed to be - Butte also had the highest death rate. In the mines of Butte, a miner's life expectancy was only ten years.

However, fate was to strike a devastating and tragic blow when on my grandfather's return his eldest daughter, my aunt, Sophia, became ill and was diagnosed with the deadly disease of consumption (tuberculosis), which was rampant throughout Ireland and was the country's biggest killer at the start of the 20th century.

Sophia sadly succumbed at the age of sixteen in 1916, which effectively put paid to any ambitions my grandfather had of returning to Montana. Sophia's tragic death, however, was not the last crushing blow to hit my grandparents and their children. Within a year of Sophia's death, infants Winnie and Cassie also died. My grandfather took the family from Edrim Glebe to live in neighbouring Mountcharles as back then it was believed tuberculosis lingered on in a house in the walls. It was several years before they returned to Edrim Glebe but it was not to prove a happy return. By 1923 two more children had arrived, James, and Margaret, but then my grandmother Mary also died of the dreaded consumption, so called because the disease seemed to consume the whole body.

There is nothing I could say or write which could describe the great sorrow my grandfather and his seven remaining children – Patrick, Dominic, my father Hugh, John, Mae, Jim and Margaret - must have felt at the time and in the decades that followed. My father never spoke about his mother while we were growing up and when we were adults we felt we could never talk comfortably about the subject with him.

Back in 1917 and aged just fourteen, amid a climate of great political unrest and much poverty in Ireland, when the final stages of the Great War were being played out on the Western Front and as he was still mourning the loss of three of his siblings, dad and his brother, Dominic [Dick], ran away to England, no doubt attracted by the endless stories of regular wages and high living.

Shortly after discovering that the pair had upped and gone, my distraught grandparents enlisted the help of the Royal Irish Constabulary in tracking them down, but it was to be another three months before they were finally discovered working in a mill in St Helen's in Lancashire, and were brought back to Donegal by their father. Dad often related the story of being fed on baked beans by their landlady for the entire three months of their sojourn in Lancashire and could never stand the sight of beans thereafter.

In July 1922, at the age of 18 and with the onset of the civil war, dad and his pal Jim Brennan, from Mountcharles, enlisted in the fledgling Free State Army at Glenties, Donegal, while in January 1923 Dick enlisted at Drumboe, Donegal. Dad mentioned very little about his experiences of the civil war, except to say that he and his friend Jim had been arrested as spies on their way to Drumboe and he also often mentioned his father keeping "small arms" in the thatch during the Black And Tans[7] period of terror in Donegal.

After their mother's death and the civil war which had left Irish society so divided and embittered, my father and his brother Dick, lured once again by the endemic tradition and attractions of emigration, and fed up with social and family friction (dad described his father, to put it mildly, as an "old bastard" and a "tyrant" who was permanently without money) an overcrowded home and no future, began to make tentative plans to emigrate for a second time. "Sure! What was there to keep them at home?" remarked the late Abbie Gallagher, a close friend and neighbour of the Carneys in

Edrim Glebe. There were no acres of land for my grandfather to sell in order to educate them or keep them busy at home; no old-school cronies, who could fiddle the system for him. His sons, it seems, like thousands more, were bred for export and were on their own and, as the old song goes, "On the one road to God knows where".

With just the clothes they stood-up-in, my father and Dick waved a fond farewell to Donegal and hit the road once again destined for England. The pair headed for Derry via Strabane and then on to Belfast, where a booking had been made as deck passengers on the steam-ship Antrim, which was bound for Heysham.

Unwittingly for Dick, it would mean permanent exile, for he was never to see his father or brothers and sisters, or indeed Donegal, ever again. Likewise, my father would never see his father or eldest brother Pat[8] again and it would not be long before he was to say a permanent goodbye to Dick.

The brothers initially headed for Rotherham, South Yorkshire, on the recommendation of friend Con Fury, who hailed from Ballydavitt, near Edrim Glebe. Their plan was to make enough money in Rotherham to enable them to then emigrate to Canada.

After leaving the then new docks facility at Heysham, they tramped the Pennine Hills, sleeping rough, before eventually arriving after three days on the march in the grey, grimy, industrial steel city of Sheffield in South Yorkshire, and then to the equally grimy adjoining steel and coalmining town of Rotherham. Writing in 1909, William Howells, an American visitor to England, had this to say about the area: "Leaving Manchester we began to climb the green thickly wooded hills and grassy leafy valleys. In the very heart of loveliness we found Sheffield, nobly posed against a lurid sunset and clouding sky, which can never be certain of being blue, with the smoke of a thousand chimneys from whatever point you look."[9]

Con Fury had found dad a job on the Retort at Rotherham's newly built power station, while Dick found work on building sites[10]. The Retort was a series of gigantic, cast-iron, bottle-like vessels used in the distillation process of turning coal into gas, and used for powering the mighty steels mills of Sheffield and Rotherham and the many thousands of homes in this industrial heartland.

The Retort was a hot and filthy job and dangerous at times too, and it eventually claimed the life of Con Fury in the 1930s. However, dad stuck it out shoveling away, feeding Dantes' Inferno amid the heat, smoke, coke and coal fumes until he was laid off during the General Strike of May 1926.

England's first and only General Strike lasted nine days, from May 4 to May 13. It was called by the general council of the Trades Union Congress in an unsuccessful attempt to force the British government to act to prevent wage reduction and worsening conditions for coal miners.

The strike is generally seen to have ended in defeat for the union and the miners but there is no shortage of irony in the fact that following it my father found work at the coalface in a mine near Rotherham.

After the fiery graft at the Retort, it was a case of "out of the fire into the frying pan" for my father, for his new job was every bit as rough and dangerous.

It has often been said mine owners at that time actually showed more compassion for their pit ponies than they did for their men. A dead or badly injured miner could easily be replaced at no cost, but a pit pony had to be bought!

Years later dad admitted his first ever shift as a miner had been a terrifying experience. Going down in the cage on Monday morning was the worst part, he recalled. The stink was enough to render anyone unconscious as a result of miners venting the weekend's excesses of beer, beef, and Yorkshire puddings. However, mining must have suited my dad in a strange sort of way. Perhaps it was the comradeship and banter which were unique features in all mines the world over. Or perhaps he saw it as a personal challenge, the sort of challenge his own father and uncles had risen to and overcome when working in the mines in Butte, Montana. More likely, and certainly more importantly for a young immigrant, mining paid better wages than any other manual work at that time, even taking into account strikes, lay-offs, lockouts and injuries.

Dad worked at Silverwood Colliery for a gangmaster who spent the entire shift sat on a box, watching the men work. If he caught a man resting he'd pick up a stone and let fly at the slacker. The Puffler, as they used to call him, was so fat that each time he bent to pick up a stone a mighty release of wind would vent from his ass.

The work was tough, but the conditions on the surface were not much better for my father.

He lived in what could only be described as a ghetto in the Rotherham district of Masborough, with hundreds of other young and not so young Irishmen and their families. The grime-coated houses, many more than 100 years old, were surrounded by steel rolling mills and associated industries which merged with the giant steel works and foundries of Sheffield, where the incessant noise of foundry steam hammers, the boiler works, the strip mills, locos, and works' buzzers continued 24 hours a day.

Masborough was an overcrowded, flea-bitten, stinking, health hazard. Its depressing red-brick houses were mainly back-to-back, two-up and two-down, which were blanketed day and night in a permanent, thick yellow toxic sulphuric haze emanating from the steel mills and chimneys. Even in the 1960s, Sheffield and Rotherham, were officially designated as the worst polluted areas in Europe. This was life in early 20th century Britain, where a decent rented house or digs were extremely hard to come by for anyone, let alone Irish immigrants.

"No blacks, no Irish, no dogs", was the sign that greeted many men looking for lodgings and things did not really start to improve until after the Second World War in 1945 when the first successful socialist Labour government came to power and took the bold initiative of funding a free National Health Service for all. They also embarked on a long-held promise of re-housing the country's deprived population still scarred from war. In time, the move alleviated much hardship poverty and ill-health for many millions of decent, hard working people.

In 1926 my father met my mother, Doris Eliza Broadhead, "and no luckier day indeed it was for him".

My mother's parents were shop owners in Rotherham. Their means were such that they were able to educate my mother privately at Moorgate Grammar School For Girls[11].

My dad met my mother somewhat unromantically while visiting her family's shop in order to buy some pipe tobacco, and the rest, as they say, is history. Within a year they were married in St Bede's Catholic Church, in Rotherham, my mother having converted to Catholicism for which she was duly ostracized by her parents. My grandparents on my mother's side were strict Church of England and had a deep, ingrained mistrust and dislike for the Irish and the Catholic faith.

"Send 'em all back in open bottomed boats" was the frequent jibe I used to hear in the 1950s and 1960s. That's just how it was then in the UK and how it had been for many, many years.

Married life for my mother and father began in a rented room in the St Ann's district of Rotherham, a run-down and rough area by anyone's standards with drunkenness and brawls commonplace events. In 1927, not long after they were wed, my sister Sheila was born. What a start to married life! The reality was that two relatively young adults, born in different countries and raised in very different circumstances had been left to make a life for themselves and their newborn daughter in the grimmest of conditions, with little in the way of cash or family support and having breached an unforgiving religious divide.

1 The Ascendancy is a phrase used when referring to the political, economic, and social domination of Ireland by a minority of great landowners, Protestant clergy, and members of the professions, all members of the Established Church (the Church of Ireland and Church of England, both being the State Churches) between the 17th century and the early 20th century. The Ascendancy is widely seen as excluding primarily Roman Catholics

2 Wikipedia, *http://en.Wikipedia.Org/wiki/Sir_Charles_Trevelyan,_1st_ Baronet#cite_note-1*

3 Great-grandfather Patrick departed his short, tragic life on January 15 1877 aged only 52 and Sophia on the December 6, 1905, at the ripe old age of 77.

4 Poitin is an illegal, home-distilled spirit, usually made from malt barley or potatoes

5 Although it is known Bridget, like her brothers and sisters, emigrated to America, no one knows what actually happened to her and like many immigrants to the US in the 19th century she disappeared without trace.

6 Daly died in New York in 1900 aged 58 in 1900. Thousands attended his funeral Mass in Butte. His obituary from the Butte Miner reads: "*A mighty oak has fallen! Marcus Daly was a man to remember. He fought his way from dire poverty to fabulous riches, a true empire builder. He was a man of extremes; a friend to his friends, to his enemies remorseless and unforgiving. Daly, a father figure, watched over his family, his friends and* *his employees with a heartfelt benevolence. He treated his employees better than most corporations of the time. More than any other man, he built the Montana copper mining industry. He was a true son of Ireland which he never forgot and helped."*

7 The Black And Tans were recruited from unemployed Great War veterans in England to combat increasing aggressive tactics by Irish nationalists. By 1920, the government had enrolled some 14,000 new police recruits. Due to a shortage of police uniforms, these new recruits were issued with a cobbled-together police and army khaki uniform, hence the moniker the Black And Tans, and they soon became notorious for their brutal suppression and violent tactics. However, as bad as the Tans were, the increased IRA campaign led to another recruitment drive in the form of the Auxiliaries, who were former British Army officers who wore the distinctive Tam o' Shanter caps and operated as counter insurgency units. The Auxiliaries were never regarded as police in the community they served in, but are remembered for their brutality and militarization of the Royal Irish Constabulary and were infamous for their cruel reprisals on ordinary Irish citizens. Donegal town witnessed much brutality during that period with the shooting dead of local men Captain Hugh Britain and volunteer James Gallagher at the Schooner bar in the town, and also the shooting dead of a young woman on holiday from England while visiting relatives in Mountcharles. The ransacking of the town by the Tans followed the killing of an RIC officer, Constable Satchwell, in an ambush in Mountcharles, not that the Tans needed an excuse to use acts of violence on the public. Paddy Gallagher, brother to James, was interned for his IRA activities. Paddy's wife was Catherine (Kate) Carney, who was born in Butte, Montana.

8 Eldest brother Pat emigrated to the US in 1921 aged 21. After a spell in the United States Army, he made his way to Holister in California where he found employment in the fruit canning industry. By 1928 Pat was dead, "Lord have mercy on him", a victim of typhoid fever. A few weeks after his death, my grandfather was informed of his son's death by the Garda as he worked in the fields overlooking Donegal Bay haymaking. The late Rene Mullhern, a local publican, told me she witnessed my grandfather sitting down on a hay stook and bitterly crying.

9 WD Howells. Seven English Cities, Harper & Brothers (1909)

10 While my father was to remain in South Yorkshire, eventually marrying my mother, Dick still had his heart set on emigration. Being a country boy, he couldn't stand the rough life of stinking, grimy industrial Rotherham, and so in 1926 he left and headed for Canada. He eventually made his way to Butte, Montana, where he found work for a short spell staying with the Carneys. However, Dick failed to settle in Butte and eventually found work in neighbouring Idaho with gangs of fellow Irish immigrants driving new rail track across the West. Dick, a jocular and lively wee redhead, was making good money with his fellow countrymen and the great outdoors suited him just fine. However, his luck eventually ran out when he was blinded in one eye as a result of a shard of steel piercing his eye and left him without work. Dick eventually arrived in New York penniless during the Great Depression of the 1930s . Dick said to my brother Terry when he paid a visit to New York in the 1970s: "I was so down and out when I arrived in New York even the dogs wouldn't bark at me". After the Depression, Dick trained as a barber and settled in the Bronx district of New York and married Ann Gilmore, who had emigrated from Foxford, County Mayo.

11 My mother was taught English, French. music, art, sewing and cooking, which she did exceedingly well. She was well known in our family circle for her culinary skills and hospitality. The belief then was that girls should be educated for motherhood and when you educated a boy you educated him to become a man. Several of my mother's paintings were brought with her to the pit house in Maltby. Alas, they didn't survive. However, her old piano did and was used for piano lessons by my sisters years later.

Miner setting a prop Rossington Colliery 1942
resembling a "hammered iron statue"

Shaft sinkers down the shaft drilling and blasting 1909

Temporary timber mine head frame

Shaft sinkers posing in the kibble ready to descend for their twelve hour shift in their quest to reach the Barnsley seam

American built Steam Navvie, and navvies near the village of Tickhill cutting the track on the South Yorkshire Joint Railway 1906

Infamous railway navvies had a reputation for drinking and fighting, cutting the track near Maltby 1906

Evictions at Denaby South Yorkshire 1902/3 as a result of the strike, dubbed the 'bag muck strikes' police were armed with cutlasses. 800 miners lost their homes. Including their families over 2,000 people were made homeless.

Irish neighbours *"That we in coming days may be still the indomitable Irishry. WB Yates "Under Ben Bulben"*
.David Emmons in his book the "Butte Irish"wrote
"Nowhere do all the factors involved in the development of an Irish working class in the West converge as they do in the copper mining centre of Butte. In population, production, and size of workforce, Butte had no rivals among mining cities anywhere in the world, and it was one of the most overwhelmingly Irish cities in the United States. Twenty five percent of the residents of Silverbow County were either Irish-born or the children of Irish-born parents, a higher percentage of Irish than in any other American city at the turn of the century. Irish Catholic families tended to be large and close-knit. Grandparents had almost as much influence as parents did on children's lives. courtesy of Lee Whitney and Ellen Crane from their book: {Images of America} "Butte"

Top: An Gorta Mor. Irish
(The Great Famine 1847)
Illustration--Searching
among blackened potato's

Right: Rare image of Dublin
Gulch and Centreville;
Butte,Montana USA. Circa
1890. 300 mines were
operating within Butte's
city boundries. Left Irish
owned Hannifans boarding
house; right the Neversweat
mine with its famous seven
stacks, courtesy Butte born,
Marie Stresser- Bley {Carney}
Spokane WA.USA.

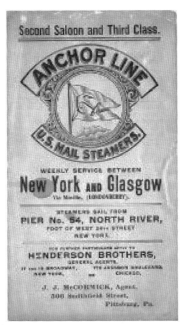

Ticket to sail circa 1900 Ships including the Caladonia picked
up passengers from the port of Derry. The majority of Donegal
immigrants left Ireland for the United States by this route.

The boys of Glencoagh National School Mountcharles Co, Donegal, left
Miss Mc Monagle, right the Master Quinn. 3rd row up 4th boy in from
right is Hugh Carney my father.

My parents Hugh
Fergus, and Doris
Eliza, Carney 1926

Rippers at work, probably one of the toughest and most dangerous
jobs in coalmining.

Inside view of the old wooden church on Morrell Street, evoking a brief whiff of damp wood, candles, incense, and the roaring of Father John Mullan.

ROACH ABBEY 1922

Annual Trinity Sunday pilgrimage to Roche Abbey 1922. Third from left is Father Vos, second from left is possibly Father Parkin.

Trinity Sunday procession at Saint Mary Magdalene, circa 1920
enlarged its possible to see Jack Towhy, the tallest man directing the
procession.

Trinity Sunday procession heading for Saint Mary's School
when it never seamed to rain.

Maltby Catholic Club football team 1927

Back row, unknown. unknown, B. Edwards, P. O' Dowd, T. Mc Cann, F. Connolly,
Middle row, Trainer T. Murphy, M. Mee, R. Fitzgerald, unkown, T. Heathfield, P.
Fitzgerald, H. Southern, J. Hansbury, J. Mee, J. O' Connor. *Front row:* J. Southern,
P. Fitzgerald, Father Vos the captain, Albert Davies, J. Marshall, G. Brough.

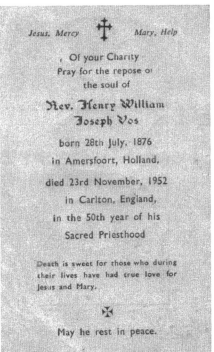

Jesus, Mercy ✠ Mary, Help

Of your Charity
Pray for the repose of
the soul of

**Rev. Henry William
Joseph Vos**

born 28th July, 1876

in Amersfoort, Holland,

died 23rd November, 1952

in Carlton, England,

in the 50th year of his

Sacred Priesthood

Death is sweet for those who during
their lives have had true love for
Jesus and Mary.

✠

May he rest in peace.

Memorial card of
Father Henry William
Vos, born Amersfoort
Holland 1876.

Laying foundation stone for the new Saint Mary Magdalen Church,
with Bishop John Heenan, and Father Patrick Coleman.

First Communion outside Saint Mary's school, teachers Mrs Meehan,
'ather Patrick Coleman, Father Christle, Miss Flanigan, Miss Finnigan.

Trinity Sunday procession 1950s Note the author having a bad hair day.

A day out at Roche Abbey, Hugh and Doris Carney, with children. Left Sheila, Patricia, {Pat} Terence, {Terry}

Trinity Sunday Men of the parish.

Trinity Sunday Ladies of the parish.

Legion of Mary:
from left, Eileen lavin, Kathleen Regan, Margaret Carroll, Eileen Mc
Namara, Nora Nockton, Kath and Nora–Cavanagh, Maureen Lavin
Front row, Kathleen Morn, and Miss Nelson.

Night at the Queens Hotel, Mick Sullivan's greyhound Pat. **Left,** Paddy
Bradish, Neil Bradish, Dennis Gildea, Leo Bradish. Terence Carney, Jim
Regan, Sean Carney, **front** Sean Doonan.

Father John Mullan, in his dotage the fire almost extinguished.

Parish Ladies The late Gertrude {Girty} Carberry and children. The Carberry's were stalwarts of Maltby's Catholic community, to her left is Mita Donnellen sister of Paddy, Mita, now lives in Australia. Gertty's husband Jim was a miner.

Coal face miners.

CHAPTER EIGHT
HEAVEN AND HELL

IN 1928, probably less than two years into their married life, my father and mother got lucky.

After working in several mines in the Rotherham and Doncaster area, dad found work in the relatively new mine in rural Maltby. It not only offered a lifetime's work but also, thanks largely to the still relatively new Model Village, much better housing and living conditions in which to raise a family.

The village now contained in the region of 2,000 terraced homes, all set in rows and concentric circles and built with monotonous red brick. But this community was a rough diamond, built as it was in an otherwise beautiful landscape and complemented by the addition of three pubs.

Arriving in Maltby with their few possessions transported by horse and dray, the family's new mining company house had all the mod cons of its day and was lit by gas (electrification didn't come to Maltby's pit houses until the 1950s). The house, built as it was on the edge of the village, also had a huge garden facing out onto beautiful open countryside where dad could grow vegetables, flowers, and keep chickens; it was sheer comfort and in sharp contrast to the dirt, grime and squalid conditions they had left behind in Rotherham.

But you can't eat the grass and the wheels of British industry had to keep turning. The men couldn't just spend their time taking in the view; they had to work to keep their families fed and even if Maltby was a vast improvement on Rotherham, a mine is a mine is a mine; pitch black, hot and sweaty and full of dangers at every turn. As my dad said: "If Maltby was heaven then the pit was purgatory."

In the early days of Maltby Main Colliery, there were between 300 and 400 men employed winning coal by pick and shovel.

Large quantities of industrial gas and coking coals as well as the world-famous London Brights were extracted and by 1935 one million tons per annum was being mined. Around about the time my father arrived in Maltby, the workforce numbered nearly 2,700, of which more than 2,200 were employed underground, the remainder on the surface, with a manager, under-manager, two overmen to every shift and 35 deputies all overseeing the show.

If working in the mine was indeed purgatory for my father, the blow was softened significantly by the company he kept.

Dad began working with lads from Ireland who were more or less the same age. They were Johnny Durkin, from Sligo; Martin Gildea (a huge man "with arms like legs", according to my father), from Tobbercurry, Sligo; John Joyce, from Galway, the second generation Irishman Tommy Giblin, and occasionally the slightly eccentric Limerick man Jack Ryan, whom many said "could shovel coal faster than any other man in the pit". These five, sometimes six, tough "sons of the old sod" had a great reputation for hard work and high wages. My dad, and I'm sure his mates would agree, judged a man by his ability to work. If he could work hard like them then he was a grand man and worthy of their respect. But I can say without fear of sounding boastful, not many men could keep up the pace with Hughie Carney and his mates.

"I would sooner lose my job than work with those mad men", said one former colleague to me years later.

Their unstinting work ethic was driven by the fact the more work they did the more they got paid, pure and simple.

From the beginning, dad and his mates were employed as "rippers" under the butty system, as it was known in some areas.

During the 19th century, coalminers were not directly employed by the mine owner but by a contractor called a "butty". He engaged with the mine owner to deliver coal at so much per ton. He employed the labour required and used his own horses, tools and equipment. This relieved the mine owner of his responsibilities for the pit or the safety of the men, leaving the butty with the simple aim of getting as much coal out as possible with the fewest number of men possible who would be willing to work for the least amount of money possible. The miners were paid daily or weekly, but not by the mine owner.

As a girl, my late eldest sister, Sheila, often recounted going to the pit yard to pick up dad's wages while he slept after doing the night shift. She recalled how the men in flat caps, with coal-blackened hands and faces, would be squatted on their haunches in a circle in typical miners' fashion waiting for the contractor to hand-out their individual wages.

Ripping was a tough and a particularly dangerous job which my father and his mates did until retirement. It involved opening up the coal face by driving tunnels (headings) with the aid of cardex shots (explosives), putting in steel roof supports (rings), track, conveyors and air bagging. In those days before the mines were fully modernised[1], it required guts and staying power to work year in, year out at 3,000ft underground in a pitch-black world with just a safety lamp or headlamp to guide you. Constant companions were the stink from the sewer-like environment, colonies of mice, salt water seeping through the rock into your eyes, dust, dirt and falling rocks, all the time spent crawling on your belly, back or sides through narrow, creaking timber propped passageways. Men were known to work naked because of the heat. Picture the scene - naked men, black with coal dust, faces and bodies streaked with constant sweat and muck, eyes twinkling in their black faces crawling on hands and knees in tunnels not wide enough to turn around in. I'll never forget those ghastly, slurry-soaked pit boots either, which I used to take to the cobbler for repair. They resembled rhinoceros hide, in colour and in texture.

All miners in the hot, deep coal mines such as Maltby added salt to their Dudley (their half-gallon zinc water canteen) in order to combat dehydration. Chewing tobacco was also a necessity some would say, as it was a substitute for smoking and helped to avoid inhaling coal dust by keeping a miner's gob full of juicy black spit. My dad's preference was Condor thick twist.

When I lived at home while dad was still working, I used to wonder why he liked to sit in the dark with just the glow of the coal fire to illuminate the room. My mother used to say he was just resting his eyes. It seems strange that a man who worked in the dark or in very poor light would want to sit in the dark at home, but it's my belief that prolonged working in bad light caused miners to suffer eye problems and that strong light agitated their eyes and it has been well documented that British and European pitmen suffered from Miners' Nystagmus, a disease caused from working in poor light.

On one occasion, while working for weeks on end in waist-deep disgusting slurry, no doubt containing a myriad of toxic chemicals, my poor old dad developed boils which covered his body from his chest down. I vividly remember the pathetic state he was in as my mother used to treat him daily with ointments when he came off shift. It's about that period, being aged about ten or 12 as I was, that I first began to realise what a shit and dangerous job he had.

Sometimes dad would recall the frequent but still frightening roof cave-ins.

There would be a loud, deep rumbling noise, like distant thunder, followed by a deathly hush as all the pit went quiet, hoping to hear sounds of life. Men hurried to the burial scene, their lamps flashing on the tunnels like an aurora. As they clawed with bare hands at the coal, rocks, and stone, hoping to find their buried comrades alive, many were in tears as they worked. Through the carnage, dead comrades were pulled out, their bodies crushed, limbs twisted and broken.

I can still remember the feeling of anxiety I had as a boy whenever I saw the vintage indigo-blue ambulance, the red cross emblazoned on its sides, hurriedly making its way out of the pit yard heading to Rotherham or Doncaster infirmaries with its brass bell urgently clanging, always hoping it was someone else's dad.

In 1942, Sligo native John Carroll, a married man with three children, was buried in a roof fall along with two other men as they worked at the coal-face shortly before the start of the Christmas holiday. It took many hours of digging before the men were released. Badly injured, they were brought to the surface on December 23.

Bridie Durkan, John Carroll's daughter, who still lives in Maltby, recalled the events to me in 2010.

She said: "The men were buried in a roof fall. In twisted contortions, my dad lay on top of the other two. They were trapped and unable to move. The man who was lying immediately underneath my dad, realising his condition was critical, mentioned that he was a Catholic, so dad suggested he make an Act Of Contrition. The man replied he hadn't been a practicing Catholic for many years and could not remember the act of contrition. 'Okay, no bother,' said my father. 'We can say it together' and they proceeded with the prayer in muffled tones.

"After they were brought to the surface, the lapsed Catholic miner sadly died in the ambulance room. My dad was brought home after being treated by the mine doctor. He was then transferred to a hospital in Sheffield and stayed there for many months. My mum visited him as much as she could. However, due to public transport being sparse at that time during the war, it was extremely difficult to get to Sheffield. We three children were only allowed to visit dad once a month, and then only from behind a glass screen.

"After two years of recuperating, dad was judged to be physically incapable to continue working underground. He received no compensation for his injuries. Had it not been for the comradeship of the miners and kindly neighbours, I don't know what mum would have done as my dad's wages and coal allowance had been stopped shortly after his accident. We relied on the odd bucket of coal from the neighbours to keep us warm and cook.

"When my dad was finally allowed to go back to work, he was given a job manning the telephones in the pit office. The wages were very poor, but at least he was safe.

"Bridie also reminded me of the times when mine owners could shut the mines down at whim when coal prices fluctuated, resulting in many Irish miners tramping to Lincolnshire in search of farm work. She said the farmers treated the Irish very badly, knowing they were desperate for the money. The conditions they lived in were dreadful, worse than that of the farm animals. "But dad came home after many weeks away, with £90 in his pocket," said Bridie. "He thought he was a millionaire."

All miners and their families without exception lived with the frightening reality that one day their husband, father, son or brother might not come out of the mine alive.

Death could come from a multiplicity of incidents and my mother and our family were no strangers to some of the accidents and indignities my father and his workmates put up with while working underground in the 100 degree gaseous humidity.

Dad had many accidents underground, the most serious being when he was buried in a roof cave-in, which resulted in him being trapped by huge rocks for many hours. While attempts were made to free him, his mates erected corrugated sheeting over him to protect him from any further rock falls.

Dad sustained a broken leg and spent a period in hospital after that accident, but throughout his time down the pit he also sustained crushed hands and feet, sprained ankles and wrists and any number of cuts[2] and bruises which were just a fact of life for a miner. Blue scars and ingrained coal dust to a miner's soft tissue on his lower eyelashes often resembled eyeliner and were the telltale marks of a miners – it was certainly no use kidding anyone you worked in a bank!

Back at the surface, miners' wives should also be remembered for the hardships and drudgery they put up with too.

Unlike families of today, miners' families were often large, and it wasn't unheard of in Maltby to have a brood of up to 16 children.

Unlike today, husbands and wives had clearly defined tasks. Mining men didn't cook, bake, do the washing, push prams, mind children or take them to school. They didn't sew, darn socks or knit woolly-jumpers. They didn't change and make the beds or help friends and neighbours in childbirth. My mother, like most miners' wives, got up in the morning to cook my dad's breakfast. In my mother's case, that meant rising at 4am in order to get my dad fed and ready to be at the pit for 5am.

Her life in Maltby, being that of a miner's wife, must have been in stark contrast to my mother's comfortable upbringing. However, she fully committed herself to being the wife of an Irish miner and all that it entailed[3]. She was an extremely proud woman who kept her five children[4] well turned out, well fed and as respectable as she could.

Not all mine workers were big wage earners and in many cases women were forced to supplement their husband's wages by doing backbreaking work in the fields, harvesting peas, potatoes or hoeing – jobs that were once the domain of migratory Irish labourers who by now were now working on the city reconstruction sites following the end of the Second World War.

Monday was traditionally washday, when every clothesline in the village billowed with the week's washing. Out came the wash tub and the three-legged ponch or posher. Water was heated in a bucket or a cast iron boiler, and was then taken outside to the dolly tub, where the washing was done before being wrung through a mangle. Cooking and baking was done on the Yorkshire range, which meant the fire was lit summer and winter, from early morning until bedtime.

The fire was then banked up with slack, ready for a stab with the poker the following morning and, as the old Irish saying goes, "out of death comes life". The cast-iron range required a weekly clean which entailed raking the old ashes out, rubbing it down with black lead then polishing until it gleamed. When the job was finished my mother was often as black as a collier herself.

What few treats there were to break the monotony were often simple and inexpensive for the women of the house and included the Sunday walk in the country lanes to a village pub, a Saturday shopping trip to Rotherham or Doncaster, or perhaps an occasional night at the cinema or a Sunday night ceili at the Catholic club.

Life was hard in coal mining villages, especially during and after the Second World War when food was rationed and luxuries of any description were few and far between. But it was not all doom and gloom, not least the fact the suffering and recurring hardship of life in a pit village for everyone engendered a great degree of fellowship, epitomised by the annual free coach trip to the seaside when a mass exodus of the whole village took place courtesy of our parents' subscriptions and the organisational skills of various club committees. This was a not to be missed event with food and drinks on the journey, a free meal in the afternoon and vouchers to spend. Truly happy days at the seaside were had by all!

1 Although the Butty system was outlawed by the Coal Mines Act of 1872 the system lingered on until the 1930s. The mines were nationalised in 1947 and conditions and safety underground swiftly improved as a result.
2 Dad worked at Dinington Colliery for a short period. In the work crew was a man called Moses who was originally from the Caribbean. One night Moses suffered a serious cut to his leg which was badly bleeding. "Moses! Tha's cut thee sen," said a young lad working alongside him. "And its red blood cumin art o thee!" "You bloody idiot," exclaimed Moses angrily. "What the f*** did you expect...

Blue blood?"

3 It was my mother who kept the link going with Donegal through correspondence with my grandfather and sisters-in-law, and on occasions it was she who took our family single-handedly on the grueling 24-hour hour

trek to Donegal, where she stayed in the old family house at Edrim Glebe.

4 After Sheila was born in 1927, Patricia was born in 1931, and Terence (Terry) was born in 1935. I was born in 1942 and Michael was born in 1945.

CHAPTER NINE
THE IRISH IN MALTBY

IN 1935, Maltby Main Colliery passed into the control of the Denaby And Cadeby Collieries Ltd, and so a report of the time said, "became a more powerful and enlightened concern", which now had under its control Maltby, Denaby, Dinninton, and Rossington collieries. (At that point of the merger, one million tons of coal per year were being mined at Maltby by pick and shovel - some enlightenment!)

As a result of the takeover, many young deputies and overmen of my dad's age were transferred from Denaby Main to Maltby colliery and were all to a man proud, second generation Irish, whose fathers had hailed from Galway, Mayo, Sligo and Cork, and who had similarly toiled underground at Denaby Main.

Up to the present time, they are still referred to as the "Denaby Irish" and we the "Maltby Irish.

" There was no talk then of the bewildering, shameful term "Plastic Paddies". Back then, the Irish-born were proud of the achievements of the second generation who were treated like the rest, with no sneers or derision. They were glad to have them in their midst; all miners were dependent on each other in the mine, whatever race or persuasion.

Maltby's Irish miners and their families pulled together, for they were a clan, be it down the mine, socially, or spiritually! They worked, played and prayed together[1].

Not that the Maltby Irish were aloof or kept themselves apart from the new incumbents, for relations between the two communities was fostered through dances and socials and eventually marriages.

Music was a common thread which perhaps more than any social activity entwined the two communities.

There were several great musicians in Maltby, such as traditional fiddle players Mary Ann Fitzgerald and Rose Murphy[2]. Both the Denaby musicians and their Maltby counterparts would gather in the social club on Sunday evenings for lively jigs, reels, hornpipes, and polkas with Mrs Murphy, Mayo man Jim Regan Snr (fiddle), Tyrone's Tommy Keenan (flute) and Peter Kerr (flute), and later in the 1950s accordionist Jimmy Morgan, from Dublin, and County Galway man Johnnie Mannion on button accordion.

The Irish workforce at the mine was growing from strength to strength, and along with the new input of deputies and overmen and a scattering of men who were recruited from the west of Ireland, like the Miskells from Galway, they were proudly contributing in no small way not only to the success of their immediate community but also the success of the colliery, the village and the region.

Leaving our house in Salisbury Road for Mass on Sunday morning, a stranger could be forgiven for thinking they were actually in Ireland as we were joined on the road by any number of Irish folk, all converging from all points of Maltby and heading for Morrall Street and St Mary Magdalene's Church.

It goes without saying that while music entwined the Irish, the church was the glue that bound the community together so very tightly.

In 1918 , Father Parkin, the first parish priest who had overseen the opening of Maltby Model Village's first temporary church in 1914, retired.

He was replaced by the kind, sympathetic Dutch man Father Henry William Vos, who was born in Amersfoort in July, 1876. A student at the Leeds Seminary, he was ordained on May 21, 1903.

Father Vos did much charitable work among the poor Irish families and many others in the village. Some say he would even give away his clogs to the needy. Father Vos was transferred to Carlton in the Goole area in 1937 before retiring in 1949. He died in 1952.

He was replaced by Father John Mullan, who was born January 1897 in St Louis, Missouri, in the USA, of Limerick parents and was ordained in Leeds in 1922.

Father Mullan stayed in Maltby until 1953 when he was transferred to Thrybergh, near Rotherham.

Father Mullan's successor was the gentlemanly Father Patrick Coleman who was born and ordained in Ballaghadereen Co, Rosscommon in 1936. Father Coleman took over from where Father Mullan left-off, overseeing the building of a new St Mary Magdalene's Church and the Catholic club. Father Coleman died in

1971 in Ireland.

My early childhood memories of Father Mullan and St Mary Magdalene's Church go back to the late 1940s.

At that period in time, we children were chaperoned and herded together by parish stalwart Johnny O'Malley into the front pews, directly under the pulpit, where inevitably we got the full blast of Father Mullan's fiery sermons. Occasionally, when I'm daydreaming and my mind wonders back to Maltby, a brief whiff of the old church, of polish, candles, damp wood and incense, washes over me. I remember the smell of Brylcream-lathered hair and the stale smell of Saturday night's stout and whisky; blue serge suits and starched-white collars, brown brogues, rosary beads wrapped around gnarled Woodbine-stained fingers, work-sore knees nestling in flat caps; wives with hats pinned down on hair-netted buns, brown stockings, strong, sturdy winter shoes and quality winter coats, even in times of hardship, and the most striking feature of the Irish - their Celtic, handsome good looks.

I recall churchgoers gathering outside after Mass for a yarn in typical Irish fashion; a tall boy pumping the harmonium-pedals for wee Minny Nelson, whose short legs were unable to reach the foot pedals; Dennis Griffin and Polish miner Ted Jeziorski, the oldest alter boys in the world; an occasional "pssst, pssst" from Johnny O'Malley and a whispered "be quiet" and Father Mullan giving his sermon, raging like a mad bull, blue veins bulging in his red neck. "Show me your friends," he'd scream at the top of his voice. "And I'll tell you what you are!" This was his favourite expression and he seemed to be pointing at individual parishioners as he said it every Sunday. Tough miners would shrink in their pews with fear as he banged his fists on the pulpit from a great height, his scarlet face by this time almost exploding with rage.

Another of his pet hates were the "Bolsheviks", whom he denounced frequently as anti-Christ heathens and heretics. He considered strikes for better conditions and pay as a Communist plot to overthrow society.

Opinions varied sharply of Father Mullan, who stayed in the village for 15 years. Many thought he was a tyrant and a bully while some thought him a loveable rogue.

Taking a child out of St Gerard's, a Catholic secondary modern school in Thrybergh close to the steel town of Rotherham, and placing him in the local non-Catholic state secondary school was to him an excommunicating offence for life.

Similarly, in her early 20s my sister Patricia went to Father Mullan in search of some spiritual advice. "I don't give advice," was his abrupt answer to her. "You sort out your own problems." As a result, Pat gave up her faith on that very day[3].

We youngsters went in fear of him as he toured the village on his two-stroke Hanstock motorbike with his jacket fluttering in the wind. When we heard him coming – "pop, pop, pop, pop" - we ran like frightened rabbits and jumped over walls or hiding behind bushes.

Joe McNicholas, who lived in the neighbouring village of Bramley, had this to say about Father Mullan: "I went to St Mary's Catholic School in Maltby, at the tender age of five and left six years later. I lived in Bramley with my parents, two elder sisters and two younger brothers. We used to get the trackless bus to the Queen's Hotel my fare was a tu'penny return, then we walked to school. I was terrified of both Father Mullan and Miss McElhinney (the head teacher in the local Catholic junior school). If you missed Mass on a Sunday you got the wrath of the pair of them and you had to remember the colour of the vestments Father Mullan wore to prove you had attended Mass.

"The old church was packed to the doors every Sunday. Most of the kids had to go on the alter. I used to hate it because I always had the odd hole in my shoes. Father Mullan was up in the pulpit preaching hell, fire and brimstone - according to him there wasn't one person in the congregation going to get to Heaven. The Mass was all in Latin and I'd hardly mastered English let alone Latin." We had a great childhood although the three-bedroom terraced house we lived in was by today's standards a slum! Father Mullan lived alone in his big house, as did Miss McElhinney. They were mansions compared with our humble abode – I could never understand that!"Father Mullan used to do his house visits on his motorbike. You knew when he was coming to Bramley because you could hear him at Hellaby a mile away. My brother, Pat, and I used to run up the meadows until he had gone. My mates used to run too - and they were Proddy Dogs (Protestants).

"At the bottom of Cliff Hills was an Italian prisoner of war camp[4].

Father Mullan used to go down early Sunday morning with his big stick to get the prisoners up to attend mass. As Frank Keetley[5] puts it in his Maltby musings, they were brought in when there was a labour shortage but they didn't last long; Yorkshire miners wouldn't have them, though Yorkshire lasses would. Frank also remarked that Father Mullan used to be a right one for the sermons. He said he once preached for a full 50 minutes at Benediction telling tales of the Irish shepherd who was brighter than any university professor. He used to go on a bit about Generalissimo Franco and on one occasion my granddad got up and tried to argue with him before he was escorted out".

In the 1950s when asked by the old social club's committee for permission to build a new club, Father Mullan's reply was "Ach! 'tis a necessary evil, but it will keep our people together."

Father Mullan hated the idea of the Irish socialising in any other drinking establishment and made no bones about telling his flock at Mass. If we, as Catholics, set foot in a non-Catholic church, for whatever reason, a funeral or a wedding, we would go in fear of being sentenced to eternal damnation. Father Mullan did indeed keep his flock together and many people were thankful for that as he was a great organiser, and it was he who was the catalyst in the building of St Mary's Junior School, which opened in 1940 after being financed by the Irish community themselves. Father Mullan and the Leeds diocese were responsible for recruiting new graduate teachers from the west of Ireland. They were Misses Corr, O'Conner, Finnigan and local girls the Fitzgerald sisters; Mrs Flannigan, Miss Housen and an Austrian, Miss Wagner.

Father Mullan, in conjunction with his short-cropped, red haired, fiery-tempered first-lieutenant, head teacher Miss Agnes McElhinney, kept a tight rein indeed on their Irish flock.

As result of Saint Mary's School being built, and thanks largely to the efforts of its talented Irish teachers and the ambitions the Irish families had for their children, the pupils began to make remarkable progress.

At the time I went to school in the 1940s, an extraordinary high percentage of pupils from Saint Mary's passed the 11+ exam, which enabled them attend a nearby engineering technical college, or De La Salle and Notre Dame Catholic colleges in Sheffield, and then later on to university.

Those who opted out or didn't make the grade were bussed to St Gerard's[6], where any semblance of intelligence fell on stony ground amid teaching methods which included favouritism, humiliation and gratuitous acts of violence from bullies and highly-strung teaching staff.

A thing that puzzled me throughout my adult life was the lack of teaching of the most basic of Irish culture and history, even at secondary level[7]. Had it not been for our own natural inquisitiveness, knowledge passed down by our parents and holidays in Ireland we would have been totally de-nationalised and just the same as the all-British Cragg School kids who stoned us and called us "catalogues" every now and again. Perhaps that's how the politicians and the clergy wanted it - to Anglicise us all and perhaps deny our history. Certainly, dancing in the school hall to the tune of The Grand Old Duke Of York and the British Grenadier will be etched on my memory until I depart this mortal sod.

Still, a large proportion of the pupils who attended St Mary's in my day later went on to have successful academic, medical and nursing and trades careers. We could also boast a professional footballer in Tommy McGoldrick, who went on to play for Rotherham and Chesterfieled, and even the singer Tony Christie, whose real name was Anthony Fitzgerald (he was born in Conisbrough but was a product of the Consibrough/Denaby/Maltby Irish triangle with a number of aunts and uncles in Maltby).

But perhaps the most remarkable - and bewildering - fact is that a staggering 13 priests were ordained from the village, the first being the late Father Joe Carroll (son of John, featured in this story), and Father Bernard Needham, now retired Canon Needham.

Both the lads were born in a time of much poverty in 1936 and were educated at St Mary's before going on to De La Salle. Fathers Anthony Towhy, Niall Cannon and Noel and Michael O'Connor were also among the 13.

Incidentally, in 1938 my late eldest sister, Sheila, was the first Irish Catholic miner's daughter to win a scholarship to the then prestigious Maltby Grammar School, going on to become a nurse and then later in life single-handedly running a successful hotel in the tourist spa town of Harrogate on the edge of the Yorkshire Dales.

In the 1950s, Maltby's Irish community was to witness another increase in its numbers; a result of another huge diaspora as thousands of Ireland's youth fled the country once again in search of work and a better life.

Ireland's economy remained stagnant at this time, underpinned by a distinct lack of technological progress.

England, by way of contrast, was buoyed by huge American loans and was experiencing a run of good years economically following a period of austerity in the aftermath of the Second World War.

Many of the young men and women who departed Ireland back then had uncles, aunts and cousins in Maltby village, while some came by word of mouth.

They are all too numerous to mention[8]. However, the majority married local second-generation Irish men and girls and flourished.

Like those who had come before them, they had a great reputation for hard work and made a good contribution to the village, the church and the Irish community. Very few of that generation would venture into the mines though, even after nationalisation and mechanisation when conditions underground began to improve, the unions were still strong and when coal was still king!

The men mostly found work in the construction industry and in the building of Britain's motorways as a nation rebuilt itself after years of bloodshed and destruction.

Prime Minister Harold Macmillan famously declared: "Let's be frank about it, most of our people have never had it so good. Go around the country and you will see a state of prosperity such as we have never had in my lifetime." He may just have been right.

---

1 Some of the families who came from Denaby, if I remember correctly, were the Fitzgeralds, Judges, O'Neills, Fallons, Hunts Regans, Morans Meehans , MacNamaras, and Sheehans, to name but a few. You wouldn't have to scratch very deep to find Fitzgerald or Hunt blood running through many a vein of the Maltby Irish.

It reminds me of an old Butte miner's story. O' Sullivan was the most common name in Butte's mines. A young fellow who had just signed on told the shift boss he'd had enough after the first shift and was jacking the job in as he feared a fall of rock might get him. "Don't worry," said Harrington, the shift boss. "If it's got your name on it it'll get you."

"That's the problem," said the young man. "My name is O' Sullivan!"

2 Rose was also a highly accomplished dancer, dance teacher and melodion player. In 1977, she made a recording for the Topic label titled Milltown Lasses – Old Time Irish Fiddle And Accordion. Her brother, Pateen Conlon, was one of the most famous traditional musicians in the USA.

3 Pat's two children are academically successful. Mara Fritzberg is an English teacher and also teaches English to BMW management in Munich, Germany, and Pat's son, Voyin, has a BA (first class) honours degree in fine arts and an MA. He is the owner of a language academy in Scarborough teaching English to European students.

4 The camp was built for British Beven Boys who were conscripted into the mines during the Second World War. After the war, it was used by Italians who worked for a short period at Maltby Main due to a shortage of labour.

5 Frank Keetley died in 2011 aged 79. He was a well-known writer and poet in Maltby.

6 St Gerard's pupils were almost to a man second-generation sons and daughters of Irish miners who had earlier in the century migrated from the near redundant Lancashire coalfields.

7 In New York in 1996, the republican George Pataki signed into law a bill making it obligatory for all school children in the state to be taught about the Great Famine, alongside the Holocaust and slave trade in America. At the signing ceremony in Albany, Mr Pataki claimed the lessons would show students "the Irish famine was not the result of a massive failure of the Irish potato crop but rather was the result of a deliberate campaign by the British to deny the Irish people the food they needed to survive".

8 It was during this period that the Maltby Gaelic Football Club was founded by Limerick-man Sean Doonan. Pat Mc Loughlan, who hailed from north Donegal arrived in Maltby about this time and married Margaret Carroll, daughter of John Carroll, who was mentioned in the previous chapter. Their daughter and John Carroll's granddaughter, Catherine, is now the head of St Mary's School.

CHAPTER TEN
GROWING UP IN MALTBY

IT is quite possible Harold Macmillan had never heard of Maltby, never mind visited this Yorkshire outpost.

But in many respects he was right; we really had never had it so good.

Maltby wasn't Donegal Bay or Galway Bay but, nevertheless, I'm sure my father and the rest of the Irish must have thought themselves lucky indeed to be living in an area such as ours.

And for us youngsters of Maltby starting out in life, it was all we had ever known.

For all the physical hardships miners and their families had to endure and despite the very real daily fears for the health and safety of my father, Maltby and the surrounding area was a fantastic place for a young boy to grow up in in the 1940s and 1950s.

It offered stability, in that we knew our parents' work was all but guaranteed for a lifetime, and there was also the wonderful sense of fraternity that a mining community generated.

The mine itself may have cast a metaphorical dark shadow over the village but the surrounding hills and lush green landscape provided a beautiful, safe environment for children to play and prosper.

We could cycle or ramble in the country lanes from early spring when the snowy hawthorn had begun to blossom and the primroses, bluebells and wild garlic were in abundance in the hedgerows. In the autumn, in the same lanes we picked blackberries and in the surrounding woods there were hazelnuts galore.

We could cavort to our hearts content in the pit woods with not a bother on us, felling the silver birch and hazel to make dens and allowing our imaginations to run wild with games of cowboys and indians. Often, we wouldn't return home until early evening when our mams had the dinner waiting.

One of the most memorable of these walkabouts was the annual September raid on the vicarage orchard at Braithwell, a neighbouring farming community.

The small hole in the dense hedge surrounding the orchard was never patched and being just big enough for a small boy to crawl through we took full advantage on hands and knees. First of all though we had to tuck pullovers into the waist of our short trousers, held tight by a snake belt, and, in full view of the vicarage house, the adrenalin flowing mightily, we thieved the most scrumptious of the vicar's old English apples and pears hanging from the sagging branches. Then, on all fours, back through the hole we crawled, weighted down, pullovers-full of the goods, waddling the mile home through the fields like expectant penguins.

Our favourite walk on Sundays in the summer was to follow the twists and turns of the beck to Roche Abbey, where we could spend the day wondering through the abbey's King's Wood, as the white swans gracefully glided over the dark, rushy lake and where we'd catch a glimpse of the big house in the distance on the Sandbeck Estate.

Often we gazed in admiration at the remains of the beautiful ruins of the Gothic architecture and stonework of the abbey, wondering and arguing just how the heck the masons got the vaulted ceiling stones and arches in place.

We dammed the beck and fished for minnows and sticklebacks, and shot water hens with our catapult. We swam in the open air Lido in our mam's homemade woolly trunks. What an itch they gave you, and they weighed a ton when we got into the freezing water on a March afternoon. By Jove! You had to be tough to swim in the Lido in those days.

Often on our daily adventures we would take a tour of the pit yard where amazingly we were able to walk about at will with not a man to bother us, as the mine locos chugged about the yard. We were able to watch the cages ascend from the number one shaft, as they brought up tubs of coal from the depths of the mine. We also watched the miners with great awe, Dudleys over their shoulders, as they waited their turn for the cage to descend into the black hole at the mighty rate of 28ft per second, their lives solely dependent on the six inch steel rope from which the cage was suspended.

The Dudley Tree never failed to capture our imaginations. It was a blackened, dead, leafless Elm - the kind which would frighten you witless on a dark winter's night - on which the miners used to throw their discarded, leaking Dudleys. To us kids, it resembled a grotesque decorated Christmas tree with scores of the zinc containers hanging from its branches.

We watched the sawyers too with their giant circular-saws cutting the pit props to size for the miners below. Many a miner's shed and palings were made from the props' leftover bark rippings and many bundle of rippings I carried home the mile or so with my dad.

In winter, when the snow lay thick on the ground we had our own ski slope. Never mind the Austrian Alps, we had Stromboli, aka the mountainous pit-tip, its height growing by the week. Discarded corrugated sheeting was used for our sled, dragging it behind us till we reached the top. Then at the count of three the whole gang of us jumped on the sheeting together and away we went like the hammers of Hell at break-neck speed, laughing our heads off, 200ft to the bottom. Good lord, Maltby was some place to grow up in. How many of today's youngsters could experience a fun-packed, adventurous childhood like ours?

When we were a little older we gave local farmers a hand with the pea harvest in July for two shillings a bag. More often than not we just acted the goat, eating more of the delicious tasting peas than we actually picked. We dropped the odd stone in the bag too, to add a bit of weight for the weigh-in. It was great fun and a means of earning a bit of our own spare cash.

At the end of the day we travelled home in the farmer's wagon, packed-full and bulging at the sides with old and young alike. Women in pinafores, old men in flat caps and shiny black worn-out suits, singing as we made our way home.

"They're picking at Epworth today, two bob a bag and big peas. Glady's Ainsworth had sent word around. Meet at Highfield Park. An open backed lorry, 30 to 40 aboard. Legs wedged against side boards. No HSE then."
Frank Keetley, Maltby Musings

In the autumn school holiday we also helped with the potato harvest but this was back-breaking work for a 14 year old. We arrived in the damp, misty early October fields at eight in the morning and waited for the tractor to spin-out the first drill. For our efforts, we were paid a pound a day and a few potatoes to take home for our mums.

Occasionally, perhaps because the farmer thought we hadn't a deal of work in us, we were put to driving the grey Massey Ferguson tractor spinning out the spuds as the pickers worked like demons on their stint, with permanently bent, aching backs.

At odd times we gave Irishman Paddy Carr a hand with his spuds. Paddy was a miner-cum-farmer who owned land at the bottom of Maltby Craggs. Paddy was a slave driver to us young lads and, to be honest, we were only there for the money at the end of the day and had no intention of killing ourselves with work.

"Work ya buggers! Bend your backs will ye!," he'd roar from a standing position on the tractor as he came up, the drills spinning out the potatoes while we lazily filled up the creels[1]. What maddened Paddy was that if we hadn't picked the drills the tractor and spinner could go no further as he would have buried the subsequent potatoes.

> *"Twin sentinels of a time gone by Cistercians dispossessed.*
> *No more Credo in unum Deum.*
> *"Just gawping tourists walking the aisles Now paved by*
> *gravestones of monks once passed"*
> **Frank Keetley, Maltby Musings.**

Previously, I recalled how the church was the glue that bound the community together so very tightly. It's influence on the Irish community and us youngsters in particular cannot be overstated.

I particularly recall the yearly diocesan pilgrimage and High Mass on Trinity Sunday at Roche Abbey, which had been a tradition since 1920. It was an especially memorable event in the Maltby Catholic calendar, when the entire parish and hundreds of worshippers from the Leeds diocese and further afield gathered in the grounds of the ruined 16th century Cistercian abbey.

The sights, imagery, sounds and smells of this great event stay with me today; religious fraternities and family groups in their Sunday finery jostled for a view of the altar and the priests; men kneeling in their caps, some sat on stumps of ancient stone columns and young boys climbing the stonework for a better view of the proceedings.

The Mass was conducted by a group of visiting priestly dignitaries dressed in their finest braided vestments. The choir consisted of a large group of trainee priests from the Catholic seminary in Newark, Nottinghamshire, who sang in the unforgettably beautiful Gregorian chant, the sound reverberating throughout the enclosed tree lined vale and the ancient ruins.

The local bus company ferried the old and infirm on the mile long trip to the abbey, at the same time hundreds were making their way from Maltby alongside the winding beck.

In the late afternoon, crowds gathered outside Saint Mary Magdalene Church in Morrell Street for a huge procession around the village streets. Dusty religious banners were brought out from cupboards looking as tatty as the church they represented.

Teachers Miss O' Conner, Miss Corr, Miss Finnigan and the head, Miss McElhinney, busily organised the children in their first Communion best. Benediction was started and the Blessed Sacrement was placed in the monstrance. Outside, the altar boys began to move down Morrell Street followed by the children, the flower strewers, with their baskets of petals, one, two, three, turn and drop.

Father Mullan would be under the canopy holding the monstrance aloft, "Sweet Sacrament Divine", then Our Lady's statue carried by the children.

Cars with loud hailers atop carried visiting priests who led the declaration of the Catholic faith, singing hymns and reciting the Rosary. Ladies of the parish in their Sunday finery, men of the parish bringing up the flank in smart Sunday suits, caps and trilbies in hand, busting for a pee after the dinnertime session at the Catholic club.

In the evening, the club overflowed with members and visitors alike. Musicians gathered for the ceili with old Jim Regan, Johnny Mannion. Mary Ann Fitzgerald, Mrs Murphy, and Peter Kerr. Beer and stout flowed mightily as Mrs Regan and the McCann Girls gave renditions of the Rose Of Mooncoin, Glenswilly and a host of other sorrowful ballads, interspersed with dancing of the Siege Of Ennis, and the Kerry Half Set. What a pity Maltby cannot be like that any more!

1 A type of wicker basket

CHAPTER ELEVEN
LAUGHTER IS THE BEST MEDICINE

FOR all the amenities, events and burgeoning material comforts that Maltby had to offer, and they were sometimes vast compared with life in the inner cities, what really made pit communities stand apart were the people, their ethics and their outlook on life.

Running through the heart of Maltby, almost as thick as the coalseam running down below, was a sense of fun and great humour.

This abundant humour was probably born out of a need to compensate for the often soul destroying work that miners had to endure, but its role in forging a community, strengthening ties and bringing people together should not be underestimated.

The stories, and the characters behind them, were numerous as one would expect from mining men, Irish or otherwise, and were constantly doing the rounds in the village.

One such tale when I was growing up referred to Yorkshireman Roley Fletcher.

Roley's heart wasn't in mine work, but you couldn't criticise him for that.

However, to compensate for his lack of interest and earning capacity, he had the hobby of collecting Second World War army vehicles.

Armoured cars and personnel-carriers were his speciality, which he dismantled on his allotment - often the scene of many a war game for us kids - and sold on for spares and scrap.

In the mine, Roley was a dataler, which in mining terms was a man who was paid on a daily rate or by the hour. He was not a contractor or piece worker and could be sent anywhere in the pit to do routine work.

Roley and six other men were on the night shift, and were sent by the County Galway-born overman John Miskell to the pit bottom to clean up fallen rock and stone.

After an hour, the seven men became bored with the shoveling, so decided to switch-off their lamps and take a nap in an out of the way place.

After two hours or more in dreamland, the men were suddenly startled by the overman's lamp flashing from the narrow, pitch-black roadway. Up jumped the seven in shock, rubbing their eyes with one hand, grabbing their shovels with the other pretending to be working. "Mr Fletcher!" shouted John Miskell sternly as he approached Roley. "I notice ye haven't a shovel."

Roley paused for a moment and before replying with a stutter: "Mmm-Mr Miskell, tha'r won't be gone two mmm-minutes darn't rooadway, www-when ar'll have sss-seven shovels!"

On another occasion, Roley was telling his workmate in a disgruntled tone how he had almost become a rich man on the football pools. "Just one team let me down," he said.

"Which team was that Roley?" asked his mate?

"Ffffff," stuttered Rowley.

"Fulham?" asked his mate.

"No! "said Roley. "Fffff…"

"Falkirk?" asked his mate.

"No!" replied Roley. "It wa'r fffff–feckin Rotherham!"

Another humorous tale doing the rounds of the village in the 1940s concerned a lecherous mine-deputy, whose name for fear of reprisals shall remain anonymous but I'll refer to him as Jack. Deputy Jack was having a passionate affair with a miner's wife, a very dangerous act indeed in a small community such as Maltby.

The bold Jack was in the habit of giving his lady friend's husband overtime in order for him to carry on with the illicit affair.

One dark winter's night, as the gas-lamps dimly flickered in the back streets of the village, Jack became even bolder and decided to pay his amour a visit at her home. After all, the husband would be at work and the coast would be clear, or so he thought!

Jack, after pondering for a few moments, cautiously gave a soft tap on the door of his "bit on the side".

As the door slowly opened, Jack was confronted with the terrifying figure of the burly coalminer husband, dressed in singlet[1] and a thick leather belt holding up his huge overhanging beer-belly and pants. Jack, momentarily tight-assed with fear, knew the game was up, but quick as a flash, blurted out apologetically: "Sorry, I've got the wrong house."

"Nay lad," said the burly miner gruffly, at the same time raising his huge knarled fist. "Tha's got reet house, but wrong time old luv!" and his fist crashed into Jack's nose, laying him flat on his back in the yard.

Irishman Mick Roddy, reputedly one of the original old-time shaft sinkers who stayed on in the village after the mine went into production, was a close drinking companion of Bill Connolly, also a shaft-sinker. They were both on the pension and were good company for each other, and could often be seen at their favourite watering hole, the Queen's Hotel, where they entertained the regulars by spinning yarns and generally having the craic. One day, old man Roddy dropped dead outside the hotel. Some say it was just old age while others blamed the excesses of the demon drink for his demise. Eventually a messenger was sent to Connolly's house to purvey the bad news.

"Mr Connolly, I've some bad news for ye" said the messenger. "Mick Roddy dropped dead outside the Queen's today."

Connolly paused for a moment, and then with reverence exclaimed: "Oh Lord, have mercy on him," and then, with wry Irish humour, asked: "Did he die going in or out the Queen's?"

"Sure, he was coming out, Mr Connolly," said the messenger. "Ach sure, dat's alright then," said Connolly.

Not all the characters in the village were of the two-legged variety. Dolly, a handsome, chestnut mare, with a brown swishing tail and mane, was owned by Mr Pickins, a dairy farmer and a true gentleman. Dolly was Mr Pickins' lifelong charge and partner in his dairy business.

Dolly faithfully plodded the streets of Maltby for untold years, placidly pulling a flat-bed milk float, laden with milk churns. Dolly knew every house and stop instinctively, and wouldn't budge till every housewife with her jug in-hand had been served by milk-maid Sadie, by means of a long handled ladle. Dolly delighted in being fussed over, stroked, and fed grass or a carrot by local children.

Sadly, by the 1950s Dolly had been put out to grass, another character of old Maltby who had disappeared from the street scene forever, replaced as she was by a motorised milkfloat and factory bottled milk.

Jack Tuohy a County Mayo man, was a steam locomotive engine driver at Maltby Main. His job was transporting the huge freight wagons of coal from the mine to various coal depots throughout the region. There are several conflicting stories of how Jack came to be in Maltby, although it was said Jack arrived shortly after the First World War, where he had been an engine driver on the battlefields of France, ferrying munitions and supplies to the troops on the frontline.

Due to his extraordinary height of 6ft 10ins, Tuohy developed a bendy-legged gait, or a gimp as it's often referred to in rural Ireland. Some of the young folk in the village referred to him as the rubber-man. Tuohy was also born with an insatiable thirst and was the dread of every Irish miner's wife in Maltby because of his natural skill in leading men astray with his native County Mayo wit and humour, coupled with the mind-boggling industrial quantities of beer he was able to consume. Mild was his favourite tipple. Even when in his 70s, it was nothing unusual to see Tuohy downing 12 to 14 pints during an afternoon session, and 20 pints on an evening. His eye never left the clock when he was in full swing, just in case he should fall behind with his quota for the session.

Despite his legendary drinking prowess, Tuohy was a gentleman of the first degree, and a respectable son of County Mayo. It was said that no-one ever saw him the worse for drink, and he rarely missed a shift of work. He was a devout Catholic and a good-living man, courteous and well dressed, and he could always be seen in a black suit, with a white collarless shirt and black flat-cap stuck on top of his long, bony, high cheek-boned face, complemented by a huge drooping poncho moustache. Tuohy addressed all women as "maa'm" and men and boys of whatever ages as "boy".

Tuohy's wife died a few years after their marriage - some say she just gave up the ghost when she realised what a gem she had in her husband. The couple had a son who departed the village at an early age who Jack hadn't seen for many years.

One day and to everyone's surprise, Tuohy brought his son into the Queen's Hotel, proudly introducing him to the regulars before they got down to the midday session. After 12 swift pints, or even more, the son fell off his barstool, blind drunk. When the regulars went to help him up Tuohy retorted sternly: "Leave him be. He can't do any harm on the floor, sure.

" Tuohy went home in disgust, leaving the regulars to bring the son home. When the lad awoke somewhat the worse for wear, Tuohy was getting ready for the evening session.

"I'll come with you, dad, "said the son, reluctantly. "No boy. You've embarrassed me enough and spoilt my day. You can't take a drink, so ye can stay here and mind the house." No one ever saw the son again. Tuohy's favourite quote, one of many, was that "three men should never be drinking together. There should always be two men talking and a third man ordering at all times".

Tuohy was also very droll. Dad and his workmates had the dubious privilege, one of many, of drinking in Tuohy's company. On one particular Sunday afternoon at the Catholic Club, pints of Guinness and Best Bitter were being swiftly necked. After untold pints of the stuff, Galway-man John Joyce, who was feeling exceedingly bloated by this time, leaned over to Tuohy, who was about to buy the next round, and said in an embarrassing whisper: "I'll have no more Jack, I'm not feeling well."

"Not well? What's the matter wit ye boy?" quipped Jack sardonically, his eyes twinkling with devilment. "Is it sick ye are John? Ye should go and see the doctor boy.

"In the late 1940s, as living standards slowly began to improve after the hard times of the war years, a salesman from a drinks firm, Hague & Company, knocked on Tuohy's door asking if he would like to try their new beer promotion. "It comes in handy four gallon barrels" he said. "Sure! Ye can leave me a barrel boy " replied Tuohy, licking his lips at the thought of it. "And when will I call to pick up the empty, Mr Tuohy?" asked the salesman.

"How far ye going boy?" asked Tuohy."

'Am just gooin darn't rooad ta Langold," replied the man, in his broad South Yorkshire accent ("Down the road" was in fact seven miles). "Ach sure! call on your way back boy," was Tuohy's reply.

Mary Hughes related this story to me about Jack Tuohy.

"Jack lodged with my Aunt Kate for a period when food rationing was on, just after World War Two. Tuohy was a very fussy man with his food and also at the times he ate it. Aunt Kate had to have his Yorkshire puddings out of the oven and his pint of beer on the table as soon as he walked through the front door. Kate found it hard at times to keep up with his demands for fresh meat.

"One day, Aunt Kate, with a twinkle in her eye, asked me to go on an errand to Doncaster market to buy horse meat. After bringing it home on the bus, Aunt Kate made a lovely big pan of stew with dumplings, with nice big pieces of the horse meat in it. Unaware of the pan's contents, Tuohy sat at the table as usual with his pint of beer in front of him while Kate ladled heaps of the steaming hot stew into his big dish. 'Whoa, Katy…Whoa, Katy'" said Tuohy nonchalantly before tucking in!"

By the early 1960s, as Tuohy got older and reached his 80s, he was unable to take care of himself, and social services took him into a care home in Rotherham.

Tuohy had many visitors from the village, but he wasn't a happy man as he was missing the Catholic Club, the Queen's and the comradeship of all mining communities.

One particular Wednesday, Tuohy absconded from the home having had enough of abstinence and the doddery old residents.

Next day, former Rosscoman man Tom McCann Sr came across Tuohy in the Queen's, looking tired, hungry, disheveled and very dry for the want of liquid sustenance.

Tom took Tuohy home where Tom's wife, Katherine, cooked him a meal. Later, after a rest and spruce up, Tuohy went back to the Queen's with Tom to have his beer desserts.

Tuohy stayed at the McCann house between closing and opening times until the Friday, and asked them if he could stay with them until the Monday, when he promised to go back to the care home.

By this time, the local bobbies were on Tuohy's trail, and had a fair idea where he might be staying.

On Saturday morning before opening time, Tuohy, Katherine McCann and her sister, Elizabeth Regan, were sat beside the coal-fired Yorkshire range warming themselves and telling the tales, as my dad used to say, when they observed two bobbies' helmets appear above the kitchen window.

Before the sharp rap came on the door the two sisters, bright as buttons and quick as a flash reminiscent of a burlesque comedy scene, told Tuohy to hide in a small pantry under the stairs which had a curtain across it, serving as a make-do door. "Have you seen or heard anything of Jack Tuohy, Mrs, McCann?" asked PC Kelly, the local bobby. "No, not at all" replied the two sisters in unison.

"Well now! Who's are the those pair of legs, Mrs McCann?" asked the second bobby, as he spotted Tuohy's black boots and skinny ankles sticking out from under the pantry-curtain. Further investigation from the two diligent law-enforcers proved it was Tuohy. The pair lifted him out of the pantry and sat him on a chair. The two bobbies knew all along that Tuohy was staying at the house, and they knew that he was being well cared for and getting his supply of liquid refreshment at the Queen's.

But the station sergeant told them that they had to clear the books for the weekend and so Tuohy was escorted back to his Rotherham care home under a cloud of depression. Not long afterwards Jack passed away. Some folk in the village said he was 82. At least his last call to Maltby, the Queen's and the McCanns was a happy one. Tuohy was given a send-off befitting his character at Saint Mary Magdelene Church, where hundreds turned out for his Requiem Mass, officiated by the Rev Patrick Coleman. Tuohy was buried alongside his countrymen and women in the Catholic section of Grange Lane Cemetery, within earshot of the Queen's Hotel and that dreaded phrase to all drinking men: "Last orders, please!"

Clifford Auckland, Anglican minister at Maltby wrote the following in his historical manuscript, Maltby. The Growth Of A Township: "There were, among others, two leaders in that early mining community who managed to maintain a social equilibrium. They were the Catholic priest at Saint Mary Magdelene, Father Henry Vos, a Dutchman, with a reputation for discipline and the use of authority, and the village constable, Bobby Lambton. At weekends the High Street near to the vast Queen's Hotel could easily take on the aspect of a film set for a Western. You could almost imagine the Sheriff rounding the corner on horseback, six-shooters firing. Father Vos could, legend has it, restore order if fighting broke out. He had an ally in Bobby Lambton. Rural Maltby never had a "lock-up", it did not need such an institution. But the new Maltby certainly did. Lambton showed great initiative. He hired part of the butcher's stable for the drunk and disorderly and other miscreants. For transport to Rotherham, he hired the butcher's pig float, net and all. It held six. Lambton was disinclined to go to Rotherham police cells with less than a full load. It is said that in order not to keep five waiting, he would always go out and find another drunk to complete the load"[2]. Frank Keetley, known affectionately in Maltby as "The Poet" and son of a Catholic miner, was born and bred in Maltby. He related the following story to me: "My mother used to tell me tales of Father Henry Vos. He was so kind hearted that that when his clogs needed repair he put one clog with one cobbler and one with another. He was a bit of a tarter (of a volatile nature). He would go on a Sunday to my Granny Keetley's house at Schofield Crescent, go up the stairs and bang on the bedroom door with his walking stick to rouse my Uncle Fred to get him to go to Mass."

In the 1950s, as emigration from Ireland again reached epidemic proportions, Maltby, as noted earlier, witnessed a modest influx of new blood into its Irish community. The following story, which is unrelated to mining but well worth noting, is an example of Irish savvy and cuteness, and relates to three young navvies in their 30s. The story had been doing the rounds of the village when I was teenager. Some said it was a pack of lies while many others swore it was true.

Corkman Mick "Dragline" O Sullivan and Mayo brothers Peter and Brendan Corcoran, who I was well acquainted with, were employed by PJ Burke, a civil engineering contractor based in Barnsley. Dragline was exceedingly fond of dogs. His latest canine acquisition which he bought from Limerick-man Paddy Bradish, went everywhere with Mick; to the pub, to work, and some went as far as to say that Pat, the greyhound, even slept between Mick and his buxom, crossed-eyed partner, Audrey, in the same bed.

The three lads had been working in a quiet countryside location, laying telephone cables and were being paid on a gang basis. Unknown to the contractor, the three had been fictitiously booking in a fourth man for the duration of the job and sharing "his" wages. No one, especially the agent, were any wiser for the scam. That is until one rainy day as the three sat in the van, word came through that the agent was to make a special visit, either to find them more work for the day or send them home.

Panic set in. The three had to think fast and prepare a story as to the whereabouts of the fourth man. As they sat in the back of the smoke-filled old van, time and their luck was swiftly running out. Dragline talked of cutting his luck and doing a runner with greyhound Pat but then a plan came to the Cork man.

Ten minutes later, Pat was sat hunched in the front seat of the van with Dragline's flat cap on his head and Brendan's donkey jacket[3] draped over him. Minutes later, and the agent had arrived.

The kettle had boiled and the agent climbed into the back of the van for a "whet of tay" before telling them to get off home due to the heavy rain and thanking them for their hard graft. He told them he was pleased with their progress and generally had the craic with them.

Pat was well behaved throughout, not making any noise as he sat motionless in the front seat taking everything in, despite it being an hour or more before the rain eased enough for the agent to continue on his rounds.

On leaving the van, with Peter walking behind him to the car, the agent reiterated his opinion of the job in progress. But it was his parting comments that Peter swore touched him most. When asked by the other two if they had got away with the fourth man, Peter repeated the agent's overall opinion of Pat.

"Peter, said the agent. "You've got a grand crew there and they obviously work and play hard but, by jaysus, the quare fellow, Pat, is it? He's one ugly fecker and very quiet too, don't you think?"

School friend Paddy Geaney emigrated at the age of 12 from Tyrone with his father, mother, brothers and sisters, and continued his schooling at St Gerard's School, near Rotherham, where a crowd of us youngsters were bussed from Maltby each day. Paddy was an extremely likeable and gregarious young buck who never stopped chattering and having a laugh. When we left school at the age of 15, Paddy drifted into unskilled work for a few years, then at the age of 18 decided to turn his hand to mining. After his initial training, he was sent working underground to gain experience with my dad and his crew of contract-rippers, who he wasn't too familiar with. Even down the pit, Paddy's exuberance didn't alter as he chattered away continuously. Maltby then was a community above and below ground, and it paid to keep your trap firmly shut and not be spreading old gossip or speaking ill of your neighbours, or you could quickly end up eating hospital food.

One afternoon, as the men were resting and having their snap (sandwiches) Paddy began bragging about his sexploits, and how he'd had his wicked way with a local girl the previous weekend. The miners listened to the tale with interest as Paddy gave a blow by blow account of his lies.

"And what was the name of this girl?" asked big John C, with a wicked look on his face.

"Ach! T'was Mary C", replied Paddy, before quickly recognising instant death in the big miner's brown eyes and clenched teeth. At that, Paddy upped and ran for his life, as John grabbed his shovel and a handful of stones and was off in hot pursuit.

The following tale was doing the rounds of the village when I was in my teens, which concerned a miner by the name of Big Bill Murfin. Maltby pit baths were built in 1939. Prior to then, miners had to walk home in their muck and bathe at home[4]. Bill had been taking a shower in the pit baths after coming off the night shift.

After removing the dust and caked-on grime from his eight hours of underground toil, Bill decided to sit down and dry himself on the wooden seats provided for the purpose.

A short time later the pit ambulance man received a vague message that a problem had occurred in the baths.

Scratching his puzzled head the ambulance man, with his first-aid bag in hand, rushed over to the baths followed by some members of management who had also been informed of the situation. They too were bewildered. "What could possibly go wrong while men were taking a shower?" they asked themselves.

On arrival at the baths, one could only describe the scene which greeted them as uproar. The whole night-shift, in various stages of undress, were rolling about with side-splitting laughter, as punch drunk ex-professional boxer Frankie Lane, the baths' attendant, lay on his back under the slatted-seating.

Big Bill was screaming out in pain as Frankie attempted to manipulate and manoeuvre Big Bill's "family jewels", which had become well and truly trapped in the gaps between the wooden slats.

With the aid of a jar of Vaseline, the ambulance man soon had Bill free, without much damage to his manhood, I should add. But, needless to say, Big Bill's pride was seriously injured for many months afterwards.

Long before the so called Irish traditional music sessions so familiar of today's pub scene, Tyrone man Tommy Keenan, a retired miner and traditional musician, performed, unpaid, at the Catholic Club every Sunday afternoon.

The club was housed within a huge corrugated-steel clad building. In its former days, it would perhaps have been storage accommodation when the new mine was being constructed. The building was raised up on huge brick pillars, resembling a cavalry fort seen in a John Wayne film. Its cladding had been blackened with years of tar coatings.

You could set your clock by old Tommy. Without fail, at the stroke of one o' clock he would produce his flute from his poacher's pocket[5]. The ancient-looking, black wood concert flute with solid silver joints was kept in an old cigar box padded with a duster.

With methodical care, Tommy would slowly assemble his treasured instrument before going up and down the scales to check the tuning. Then, with a tap of his foot, off he went like a bird taking flight, his supple blue-scarred, mine-damaged old fingers darting over the flute's apertures and producing a beautiful timbered tone as he soared through infectious, historic, foot-tapping jigs, reels and hornpipes in his unmistakable Tyrone style of playing.

No one paid attention to Tommy as the club buzzed with an incessant jumble of Irish accents interspersed with excited shouts and laughter as the Irish card game of 25s and dominoes were played on the beer-stained pine tables. The tables were shunted end-to-end along the length of the club's exterior walls, where the heat, dust and dangers of the week's mine work, the union's politics and horse racing would be discussed over hundreds of black foaming pints of stout and best bitter.

In the bad old days, the club had often doubled as a food kitchen in times of need, during strikes and lockouts or when mine owners in their wisdom could shut the pits down when prices of coal fluctuated. The club really was the centre point of Maltby's Irish community.

Not a female dare venture into the club during the Saturday or Sunday dinnertime session. Their place was shopping or cooking the Sunday dinner. Barman Bill Kennedy, just like a fireman, kept the pumps manned, the beer flowing and the men supplied with copious amounts of the heady stuff.

"How's she cuttin'?" (a reference to haymaking), the men would greet old Tommy, who'd be rigged out in his Sunday best attire of black cap, black suit and matching waistcoat, white shirt and tie, and a nice shine on his black lace-up boots. "Ach, fair to middlin', sure" he'd reply unassumingly, as he sat at his regular seat at the door and as the reek of pipe and cigarette smoke, beer and stout, and an occasional whiff of the hard stuff, wafted on through.

On entering this murky old den, the fumes would almost knock you over. There sat my dad playing 25s or dominoes with his workmates, The Silent Five as they were known in the village, as they worked and socialised together without two words being spoken between them. When my brother, Terry, and pal Denis Gildea or any of the other young fellows walked into the club the Silent Five eyeballed the lads, who knew exactly what the men wanted without a word being spoken. It meant: "Go to the bar for more beer".

In the middle of this sanctuary from toil and danger was a large pot-bellied coke-burning stove, its rust-coloured flue pipe meandering crookedly up through the weary buckled fibreboard ceiling. In winter, the stove was constantly stoked, glowing bright red and spilling red-hot cinders on to its stone slab hearth.

Near the entrance to the club, on the dingy, nicotine-stained yellow walls, hung a magnificent life-size oil painting of our patron, Saint, Patrick, in green and gold robes and bishop's mitre, snakes at his feet cowering in petrified terror of his golden crozier. In his right hand, he held a shamrock, symbolising the Holy Trinity, all surrounded by a broad ornate gilt frame.

As 2.30pm approached, barman Bill bellowed from behind his serving hatch, cum-bar: "Time lads, please. Time to go home!" It was a signal for a mighty stampede of panicking men, striding to the bar clutching arms and fistfuls of empty glasses, in anticipation of a last fill-up.

It was also a signal for Tommy to cease playing, to put the old flute back in its box and slowly meander home for Sunday dinner.

1 A cotton vest with short sleeves and chest buttons.

2 Clifford Auckland loc cit

3 A short, buttoned, unlined work coat, usually in black or dark blue, some having a bright yellow waterproof patch on the back.

4 Some of the original homes in the Model Village were still without a bathroom and so the miner and his family would use a zinc bath, which their wives or mothers had prepared before by boiling buckets of water in the cast-iron boiler, located in the scullery. If children were around the house, they would be sent out to play in the garden or yard. Then with the door securely locked, dads would scour away at the black grime and sweat as they sat contentedly in front of the kitchen fire. "Scrub me back love" was the traditional request in many a miner's kitchen. Long after the baths were installed at the pit, some men continued to bathe at home because of comfort offered by the kitchen fire, or perhaps it was just down to modesty.

5 It was a large pocket sewn into the inside of a man's jacket and was a means of concealing his stash, such as a rabbit or a pheasant poached from Lord Scarborough's estate, and possibly a shotgun.

CHAPTER TWELVE
"I'D DO THE SAME AGAIN"

AFTER a lifetime of breathing in coal and dust down the mines, my dad contracted the often debilitating lung disease pneumoconiosis and was eventually retired with a pathetic, measly pension in 1963 at the age of 60.

The National Coal Board doctors were not much better than mine owners in some respects; it was they who tried to put his lung problem down to bronchitis when he had been breathing in coal dust on a daily basis for almost 40 years.

By this time, dad's mates had also succumbed to the strain of a lifetime working underground and they all retired about the same time.

There was no gold watch or golden handshake for them, but my dad had no bitterness or regrets about his life in the mines, far from it. "I'd do the same again," he often said, which is testimony to the fine people he worked alongside and the community we lived in.

Although very resourceful and a keen gardener with a huge garden to tend, dad couldn't come to terms with retirement. He just didn't have enough to do, especially in the winter months.

Sisters Sheila and Patricia and brother Terry were by this time living in Scarborough, the two girls successfully running their own hotels. Terry, a skilled machine-tool engineer recently back from the hard-rock mines of the Canadian north-west territories, was also fully employed. In 1963, aged 21, I decided to up sticks and head for the coast too.

Perhaps it was because of her upbringing, but my mother always had her sights set on a better way of life rather than ending her days in Maltby. My dad didn't take much persuading and once a decision was made things moved fast. They were "on the pigs back" as they say, and with help from my brother and I and my dad's savings the pair took the extremely brave step and bought a guesthouse in Scarborough.

Ancona 113 Columbus Ravine had six bedrooms but needed a lot of work to bring it up to scratch, including plastering, plumbing, wallpapering and painting.

However, with my experience and contacts in the building trade and help from brother Terry, the guesthouse was up and running for the summer season of 1964.

Mam and dad continued running the guesthouse flat-out throughout the busy three to four months season, catering for up to 14 guests on a bed and breakfast and evening meal basis, until they were nearly in their early 70s. A remarkable feat indeed for a retired Maltby miner and his wife[1]!

My mother fitted well into Scarborough life. She had the girls on hand for company and advice on catering, and soon made friends through the church.

However, if truth be told, dad didn't fare so well. Even though he had his family around him and was naturally an outgoing, gregarious Irishman, he was lonely and missed the company of his old mates, their humour and generosity. He missed the characters, the Catholic Club, the Queen's Hotel and mining men in general.

Scarborough folk, although many of them hailed from South Yorkshire, were just not the same kind of people. At first, dad didn't appreciate that he'd come to live in a Tory town, among hoteliers, guest house keepers, farmers and fishermen who would often bite the industrial worker's hand that fed them over the decades (I refer to their non support for the miners' strikes of 1972 and 1984 and the steel workers' strike of 1980).

In 1972, mam and dad sold Ancona making a handsome profit, and with the residue bought a small, three-bedroom house in the sought after Victorian Mayville Avenue.

Sadly, dad died in 1978 of stomach cancer and a year later mam bought a flat overlooking Peasholm Park in the town where she lived until she too succumbed to cancer in 1994.

My father had certainly come a long way in every sense since his childhood days in Donegal at the start of the 20th century. He'd lived through two world wars, seen man land on the moon and through sheer bloody mindedness and hard graft traded in the poverty of Ireland for a prosperous and peaceful retirement by the seaside in tranquil, beautiful North Yorkshire. Few would argue he had earned some time in the sun after years and years spent in the pitch black below ground.

He may have missed his mates but at least he had his memories; of bravely leaving behind his family and his homeland in search of something better, and of living and working alongside the "superhumans" as described by Orwell.

The journey the thousands of Irish like my father had travelled deserves to be recognised and celebrated. Their stories, achievements and everyday heroism should never be forgotten.

Paistin Fionn (The fair haired youth)

So you left our glens and our fishfull streams,
To follow the lure of your boyish dreams:
Through the lonely cities you wonder long,
Far from the moors and the blackbird's song.

Has the world been good to you, Paistin Fionn?
Has the yellow gold you sought to win
Been worth the toil and danger dared?
Has plenty blessed you, and sorrow spared.

Ethna Carbery[2]

1 Dad instilled a fierce work ethic in us, even today, being over 70 years of age, I still look over my shoulder metaphorically to see if he's there
2 The FourWinds of Eirinn, Ethna Carbery, MH Gill & Son (1906), Page 18

POSTSCRIPT

Thousands upon thousands of young Irishmen and women, just like my father and his father before him, had been conditioned for emigration. Every single one had a unique story to tell, but each story would be bound by a common thread knitted together by the three strands of poverty, tragedy and an overwhelming desire to seek out something better for a life.

In researching the story of my father's life and those of the "forgotten Irish", I heard many similar tales of brave immigrants who weren't prepared to settle for what hand life had dealt them and in doing so not only changed their lives but those of their children, grandchildren, great grandchildren; generation after generation after generation who all benefited in one shape or another from their ancestor's bravery, sense of adventure and determination.

Mary Hughes, now in her 80s and a Maltby resident, was one of nine children. She related to me her father's experiences of emigration

She said her father, Jack, who was born on the July 1, 1901, near Foxford, County Mayo, emigrated to England at the age of 15.

On arrival in Liverpool in 1916 aboard a Dublin steamer, groups of anti-Irish protesters were laying in wait and began to stone them as they disembarked from the ship. Apparently, they believed the Irish were taking the jobs of Englishmen[1], but it must have been a frightening experience for such a young lad whose only crime was want of better. Jack must have been tempted to take the first ship back to Dublin, but the fact that he didn't merely underlines just how bad things must have been in Ireland.

"Dad and his pals set out on foot, some without shoes, with little or no money and headed for Lincolnshire to work at the harvesting on the county's lush, rich farmlands," recalled Mary.

"An experience which stuck in my dad's mind was during the long march they stopped at a house to ask for water and were told to go away. Dad couldn't believe it had happened. In Ireland it was natural to give a stranger a drink of water and/or a crust in every house.

"Eventually as they worked away at the harvesting under very bad living and working conditions, stories were going around on the Irish grapevine of good money to be made at Cadeby and Denaby colliery in neighbouring South Yorkshire. Dad got work in the mine and eventually met his future wife, Helen Noughton, the daughter of Galway parents.

"In 1928 like many other Denaby Irish they moved up to Maltby, as the pit and the village held better prospects. We lived in the Model Village overlooking The Crags and set in lovely countryside.

"Dad's brother was a migratory farm worker and from about 1931 used to call to see us every year on his way home to Ireland with the money he'd made, which kept his family over the winter, after working the season in Lincolnshire."

Mary's father died in 1974. Many men didn't live much beyond their 70s. Working in the pit took its toll on all of them.

Just as all those who left Ireland were all spurred by poverty, tragedy and the desire for work and a steady wage, so all the Irish of my dad's generation who made their lives in Maltby had subsequently the same shared stories to tell of hard grinding work, racism and religious bigotry upon.

John Davies, who was born in Maltby, related briefly his grandfather Patrick Gibney's experiences after leaving home in Killkerren, County Galway, aged 17.

Eventually, like thousands of other spailpin[2], Patrick found seasonal work harvesting on farms in the Warrington area, and later a mill at Renishaw in Lancashire.

Patrick's first experience in mining was at Denaby Main Colliery and some time later at Maltby Main, after hearing by word of mouth from other young immigrants of South Yorkshire's mining bonanza.

Martin Gildea, dad's long time workmate and drinking partner, first came to Maltby in the 1920s, perhaps following the same harvesting route as most of the Irish in Maltby.

Martin later left for the United States before returning to Yorkshire in 1933 to work at the pit.

John O' Neil and his wife, Roseann, were Martin's in-laws. John O' Neil came to Maltby from Denaby Main to sink the shaft. He recounted his experiences of the shaft being sunk when large quantities of water oozed from the shaft walls due to what is known as the green sands formation. The conditions were dreadful, he said. Nellie Gallagher's parents, Tom and Catherine, emigrated from Swinford, County Mayo, just a year after they were married in 1924. During that period, Ireland was in an unsettled and divided state after the civil war. They no doubt heard on the Mayo grapevine of South Yorkshire's mining opportunities. Tom eventually got a job at Maltby pit and for a short period the pair lived in Oldcoats, about five miles from Maltby. Soon a company house was made available for them at Norfolk Place, where they spent the rest of their lives. Daughters Nellie, Margaret and Kate were good friends of my sisters. Margaret married Irishman Bill Kennedy and for many years the pair were stewards of the Catholic Club. Kate went into nursing. And Nellie was a teacher and magistrate who married Mayo man Tom McHale, a construction worker.

Retired detective inspector Tim Miskell, who was born in the village, spoke about his family's long association with Maltby. These are his words.

"My dad John came across from Galway, a place called Newcastle, near Augrim, in 1931 at the age of 14 to join his father at Maltby pit. The first Miskell, to arrive had been Tommy Miskell, my grandfather's cousin. He was a pugnacious little man with a big heart. Old Tommy had been coming over to England for years doing casual labouring work here and there before eventually settling in Maltby. I'm led to believe that during the years of the Great War, Tommy and my grandfather skedaddled back to Ireland to avoid being conscripted into the British Army. Good job they did too!

"Back in Ireland, grandmother stayed with an ever increasing family. Beneath my dad was Tim, who was younger by about a year, then Mick, Kitty, Peggy, Nora, Babs, Paddy and Tessy. I believe that the last two were born in Maltby as the family slowly moved across. Each boy in turn was found work at the pit.

"I recently heard a poignant story about my dad as a 14-year-old boy. My grandfather was determined to get dad down the pit and earning money - grandfather was only doing what he was told by my grandmother. Anyway, Tommy being senior was asked to sort my dad out with a job through his contacts at the pit. Tommy begged grandfather not to send him down as he had in mind a job as a carpenter, but it was not to be, and in tears old Tommy took my dad for his first day at the pit.

"I was born in 1956 by which time my dad was nearly 40. He had gone through the shot firing, deputy, and overman's exams. He said that life changed for him when he became a deputy. Prior to that he could take a day off when he felt like it, lazing in the sun on The Crags or even take a trip to the seaside on his motorbike.

"I remember my time as a kid in Maltby as one where you always felt safe. You couldn't do anything without your mam finding out and you'd end up with a clip for something later that came as a complete surprise. Everyone knew everyone else. All the men who worked in the pit drank in the Miner's Institute or the Catholic Club. All the mams stayed at home and the house, particularly on Sunday after Mass, was always occupied by guests, mainly female, as all the men had gone to the club before 2pm dinner. Now that was something. All the business with Yorkshire puddings, joints, tomatoes, sausages. All done to a tee in the fire cooker.

"I think I left Saint Mary's School aged 11, passed the eleven plus, and went to De la Salle College. Great hopes didn't come to much and I left at 16. It was the police at 18 that sorted me out, and I stayed for a fulfilling career, retiring in 2005. Most of my service was as a detective and when I retired I was a detective inspector."

The late Michael O'Conghaile (Michael Connolly) was born in the Aran Islands, off the coast of County Galway.

As a young man in 1944, Michael decided to head for London for a short holiday with relatives who originally hailed from the Islands. Mick, as he was known in Maltby, decided to stay in England and found work with a London-based overhead cable contractors. He was posted to West Melton and then to Maltby. Mick had no English when he arrived in Maltby but because of its large Irish community that proved not to be a problem. Mick eventually married Kathleen McCann, daughter of Tom McCann and after a spell in the pit he spent his working life in the construction industry.

Mick was a big, easy-going man of typical Aran fashion and he often took a drink with my dad. He had a kind word for everyone he met. He was a true son of the Aran Islands, an area which my wife and I are very familiar with, my wife hailing from Indreabhan Connemara.

Michael McCann also spoke about his father Tom's emigration to England at the age of 14. These are his words.

"My dad Thomas was born in October 1900 in the village of Lissacul, County Roscommon. He was the third of seven children. Dad was a bright boy and did well at school, passing the equivalent of the 11-plus exam. In 1914 dad left home and headed for England, staying with his mother's brother, Bernard McDonald, who was a policeman in Ashton, in Makerfield, Lancashire.

"After three to four years staying with his uncle doing various labouring jobs, dad found work in the Wigan area in the mines, telling the bosses he was 21 in order to gain a man's wage. Dad worked there for two years until he heard about the mines in South Yorkshire, which prompted him to move to Denaby Main Colliery, not far from Maltby, After a spell at Denaby, he then transferred to Cadeby, and from there to Maltby Main, where he met his future wife, Kathleen Hunt, who was also of Irish descent. They were married on March 1, 1925. Over a period of 12 years they had eight children. Dad was interested in politics and in 1927 was elected on to the local council (Maltby Urban District, I presume). This was unusual because Irish Catholics were not allowed to stand before 1929. Dad carried on working at the pit while assisting Rother Valley MP Ted Dunn, writing his political speeches and accompanying him on various meetings.

"Ted Dunn suggested to my mother that dad was MP material. She asked what it would entail and was told it would mean dad having to spend some time in Westminster, which she objected to and he didn't go any further with it. Also at this time, he was steward at Maltby Catholic Club. This was an interesting time as most businesses had no cash, so my father ran a credit or slate business, and accounts were paid each week. It meant he had direct access to butchers, bakers, greengrocers and the opportunity to acquire goods that weren't so readily available. These facilities lasted till he passed on. He also did accounts for all the clubs and some businesses in Maltby.

"They lived with Dr Twigg, in the last cottage on Millindale. My mother was housekeeper for Dr Twigg and my father ran a lip down the pit with a team of four to five men, my father paying them accordingly. I asked him did he object to the mine being nationalized and his position being lost. He said he thought it was a good thing, as not everyone was in good health at the time, and therefore this gave a chance for all unemployed people to be employed and Maltby was a happy place to live. Wives had a regular income, husbands could take them for a drink or go socialising, and life improved 100 per cent.

"As we were all starting to grow up, I was planning to pay a visit to Ireland and asked my dad if he would like to accompany me. He said when his mother died in 1939 he went to Liverpool to get the boat to Ireland to attend the funeral, and while at the docks the police informed him that he could go but it was unlikely that he would be able to return to England. He believed the reason was because of continuing IRA activity.

"In 1946/7, his father died but because he had been injured at work, sustaining spinal injuries and losing a finger, he was unable to attend the funeral, which broke his heart.

"He told my mother when he couldn't bury his parents he would never go to Ireland again[3]. That was his principle right or wrong, and he stuck by it. He also told me that England had been very good to him and most other Irishmen as well. He had achieved a full and interesting working life and looked after my mother with love and care till she passed away.

"Dad died in 1975. He wasn't a saint but he was a good dad. He always gave us good advice and he left money in the bank for each and all of his children."

James Regan Snr, a native of Ballintober, County Mayo, which nestles below the Partry Mountains, left his home and parents aged 14 and made his way to Liverpool to sign on with a shipping company. Jim lied about his age, as many young lads did. He was a tall man when I knew him in the village, and due to his height it would perhaps be easy enough to make out he was 16, 17 or 18 in order to receive better wages. Ironically, however, when Jim was approaching retiring age he sent for his birth details in Ireland and was shocked to discover he was three years older than he actually thought he was. Jim began his mining career at Silverwood then at Denaby Main where he met his future wife, Elizabeth Hunt (the sister of Kathleen who married Tom McCann). Jim and Elizabeth moved to Maltby in the 1930s. Jim was a noted fiddle player in his time and Elizabeth a truly fine singer, which indeed all the Regan children were. Jim ended his mining career at Harworth Colliery before later retiring from the Royal Ordinance Factory close to the mine at Maltby.

1 On Easter Monday 1916, several hundred volunteer Irish soldiers crowded into the massive GPO building in the centre of the Dublin and proclaimed an Irish Republic, holding out for six days against the might of the British state. The leaders of the rebellion were all executed and many rebels were killed. But so too were more than 100 British soldiers, which stirred much anti-Irish sentiment in England.

In later years, this anti-Irish sentiment would often rear its head. Dad recalled a pit-top ballot at nearby Thurcroft Colliery in 1937 when the miners voted solidly against allowing immigrants – presumably Irish workers – to work at the pit. The miners feared the import of cheap labour by the colliery companies would drive down wages.

2 A Spailpín, Spailpeen or "wandering landless labourer" was an itinerant or seasonal farm worker in Ireland from the 17th to the early 20th century.

3 As a result of the British Nationality act of 1948, citizens of Eire lost British subject status automatically on January 1, 1948, if they did not acquire citizenship of the UK and colonies. Persons born before this date and not in receipt of a British passport trying to re-enter the UK after visiting Ireland for whatever reason would be classed as an alien and barred from re-entering the country. Furthermore, to the rural Irish, land ownership was a covetous, passionate issue, as many of us have experienced at one time or another. The inheritance law in Ireland dated back to Norman times, whereby the eldest child in a family or the first male had exclusive rights to his father's land, farm and property on death. For successive children, this meant emigration was their only option, made all the more worse as they watched helplessly from afar as their feckless elder brother wasted away his inheritance. As a result of the law, many men and women felt unable to return to Ireland and many Irish men of my dad's generation in Maltby never returned home after their parents' deaths.

Index

ILLUSTRATION CREDITS

1 Miner setting a prop, courtesy of M Bowyer; coal shop collection.

2 Shaft sinkers 1909 courtesy of Pete Clements.

3 Temporary mine head frame, Pete Clements.

4 Shaft sinkers posing in the Kibble, Pete Clements.

5 American Steam Navvie, courtesy of Tickhill Historical Society.

6 Infamous railway navvies, Tickhill Historical Society.

7 Miners being evicted at Denaby 1902/3 courtesy of Dr Charles Kelham Doncaster library Archive.

8 Irish neighbours posing for photograph, courtesy of researchers Lee Whitney and Ellen Crain, at Butte Silver Bow Archives, from their publication {Images of America } 'Butte'.

9 Searching for potatoes in the famine of 1847, courtesy of Steven Taylor: sttaylor@vassar.edu: Illustrated London news.com ref the famine.

10 Rare panoramic view of Dublin Gulch, 'Butte' Courtesy of Marie Bley Stresser, {Carney} Spokane WA. USA.

11 Ticket to Sail anonymous.

12 The boys of Glencoagh. The late Dominic {Dick}Carney Long Island New York.

13 Hugh and Doris Carney. Terence Carney.

14 Rippers at work M, Bowyer.

15 The old Saint Mary Magdalene's church, John Davies.

16 Annual pilgrimage to Roche Abbey 1922 John Davies.

17 Trinity Sunday procession 1920, John Davies.

18 Trinity Sunday, when it never rained. John Davies.

19 The Catholic lub football team 1927, John Davies.

20 Memorial to Father Vos, John Davies.

21 Laying foundation stone, John Davies.

22 First Communion Saint Mary's school. John Davies.

23 Trinity Sunday procession 1950s. John Davies.

24 Day at Roche Abbey, courtesy Terence Carney.

25 Trinity Sunday men of the parish, courtesy of Julia Stuart.

26 Trinity Sunday ladies of the parish, Julia Stuart.

27 Legion of Mary, courtesy of Michael Mc Cann.

28 Pat the dog from the story, photo from author.

29 Father John Mullan, Michael Mc Cann

30 Trinity Sunday ladies, Julia Stuart.

31 Coal face miners 1942 M Bowyer.

List of Irish miners

Before 1950

Hugh Fergus Carney miner: John Carroll miner: Bill Connolly shaft sinker miner: Patrick Connolly known as digger, shaft sinker & miner: Jim Cavanagh miner: Paddy Carr miner & smallholder: Tom Mc Cann miner: Jim O' Conner the poet & miner: Jim Mc Clean miner & livestock dealer: Jim Burke miner: John Durkin miner: Jim Mc Dermott miner: Martin Duffy Miner & school caretaker: Jim Mc Evilly miner: Jim Foy miner: Pat Farrell farm worker: Jim Fallon miner: Jim Fahy miner: Mick Flannery miner: Eddy Fitzgerald miner: Jim Fitzgerald miner: Paddy Fitzgerald miner: Mick Fitzgerald miner: Martin Fitzgerald miner: Johnny Fitzgerald miner: Johnny Giblin miner: Tom Mc Goldrick miner: Paddy Gibney miner: Tom Gallagher miner: Jack Griffin miner: John Geraghty miner: Martin Gildea miner: Paddy Groegh miner: Joe Gannon miner: Paddy Higgins miner: Jack Hughes miner: James Hunt miner: Peter Kerr miner: Johnny Judge miner: Tommy Keenan miner: & mobile fish & chip shop owner: William Lyng miner: Jim Kenny miner: ?Lavin miner: John Joyce miner: Mick Mee miner: Tim, Mick, & John Miskell miners: Tom O'Malley miner: Johnny O'Malley miner: Paddy Moran miner: Jim Mannion the poet miner: Luke Noughton miner: Jim Mc Namara miner: Des, Nolan miner: Mick Prendergast miner: Paddy Murphy miner: Mick Roddy shaft sinker miner: Jim Regan miner: Mick Regan miner: Jack Ryan miner: Bob Sheehan miner: Jack Tuohy loco driver: Jim White miner:

Last but not least Jim Carney, occupation farmer and a gentleman.

1950s

Diaspora

Jim Allen: Paddy Byrne: Paddy Connole miner: Mick Connolly Aran Islands, miner building worker:: Peter and Brendan Corcoran. Joe Corkery: John McCann contractor: Harry O' Conner: Jim Conlan: Charles Devine: Mick Donnellan: Martin Doran: Aidan Durkan: Pat Durkan: Jim Dunphy miner construction worker: Mick Desmond miner: Eddie Dermody; Jim Mc Dermot: Pat Mc Dermot: Mick Frain: Frank Flynn: Pat Flanagan: Harry O'Flaherty: Pat Gillan" Joe Green: Paddy and Sean O'Geoghan: Eddie Keaveney miner: Gerry Leahy: Seamus Lavelle: Pat Mc Loughlan: Pat & Larry Lowry: Micky Lynch miner: Paddy Tom Mick & Johnny Mannion: Jim Murphy: Aloysius Mc Namara miner: John Noone: John O' Neill: Paddy & Martin Rabbett: Paddy Quinn: Tom Riley: Mick O'Sullivan: Pat Smythe: Terry Sayers miner & ambulance man: Jack O' Toole: Tommy Tracey miner & ex Irish army: Luke Tuohy miner– husband of Miss O'Conner: Mick Tom and Jimmy Walsh: